First World War
and Army of Occupation
War Diary
France, Belgium and Germany

55 DIVISION
164 Infantry Brigade,
Brigade Machine Gun Company
19 February 1916 - 28 February 1918

WO95/2924/2

The Naval & Military Press Ltd
www.nmarchive.com
Published in association with The National Archives

Published by

The Naval & Military Press Ltd

Unit 10 Ridgewood Industrial Park,

Uckfield, East Sussex,

TN22 5QE England

Tel: +44 (0) 1825 749494

www.naval-military-press.com

www.nmarchive.com

This diary has been reprinted in facsimile from the original. Any imperfections are inevitably reproduced and the quality may fall short of modern type and cartographic standards.

© **Crown Copyright**
Images reproduced by permission of The National Archives, London, England, 2015.

Contents

Document type	Place/Title	Date From	Date To
Heading	WO95/2924-2		
Heading	55th Division 164th Infy Bde 164th Machine Gun Coy. Feb 1916-Feb 1918		
Heading	War Diary Of This Coy, For Month Of February 1916		
War Diary	Saulty	19/02/1916	24/02/1916
War Diary	Le-Fermont	25/02/1916	29/02/1916
Heading	164 M G Coy Vol II		
War Diary	Fermont	01/03/1916	31/03/1916
Heading	164 Bde M.G. Coy Vol III		
War Diary	Fermont	01/04/1916	13/04/1916
War Diary	Le Fermont	14/04/1916	31/05/1916
War Diary	Gouy In Artois	01/06/1916	18/06/1916
War Diary	Daineville	19/06/1916	30/06/1916
Heading	164th Brigade 55th Division. 164th Brigade Machine Gun Company July 1916		
Heading	War Diary Of The 164th Inf. Bde. Machine Gun Company 55th (West Lancashire) Division For The Period 1st July 1916 To 31st July 1916		
War Diary	Daineville	01/07/1916	12/07/1916
War Diary	Barly	12/07/1916	30/07/1916
War Diary	Near Troneswood	31/07/1916	31/07/1916
Heading	164th Brigade. 55th Division 164th Brigade. Machine Gun Company August 1916 Account Of Operations Attached		
War Diary	In Trenches Near Trones Wood	01/08/1916	07/08/1916
War Diary	Guillemont	08/08/1916	12/08/1916
War Diary	Near Bonafay Farm	13/08/1916	14/08/1916
War Diary	Mericourt	15/08/1916	19/08/1916
War Diary	Cahon Somme	20/08/1916	31/08/1916
Miscellaneous	Operation Report Of 164 M.G. Coy	08/08/1916	08/08/1916
Miscellaneous	Left Section		
Heading	War Diary Of 164 Machine Gun Company 1st September To 30th September 1916		
War Diary	Camp Near Albert Amiens Road	01/09/1916	06/09/1916
War Diary	Quarry At Barnafay Wood	07/09/1916	10/09/1916
War Diary	Delville Wd.	11/09/1916	13/09/1916
War Diary	Becordel Ribemont	13/09/1916	16/09/1916
War Diary	Buire	16/09/1916	16/09/1916
War Diary	Becordel	17/09/1916	17/09/1916
War Diary	Quarry	18/09/1916	18/09/1916
War Diary	Mametz	18/09/1916	19/09/1916
War Diary	York Tr. Nr Longueval	20/09/1916	25/09/1916
War Diary	Switch Tr. Nr. Flers	25/09/1916	28/09/1916
War Diary	Mametz	28/09/1916	28/09/1916
War Diary	Dernancourt	29/09/1916	30/09/1916
Heading	War Diary Of 164th M.G. Coy For The Period 1st To 31st October 1916		
War Diary	Dernancourt	01/10/1916	01/10/1916
War Diary	L'Etoile	01/10/1916	02/10/1916
War Diary	Poperinghe	02/10/1916	04/10/1916

War Diary	Brandhoek	04/10/1916	14/10/1916
War Diary	Ypres	14/10/1916	22/10/1916
War Diary	Kaaie	23/10/1916	30/10/1916
War Diary	Brandhoek	30/10/1916	31/10/1916
Heading	War Diary Of 164th Machine Gun Coy For Period 1st November To 30th November 1916		
War Diary	Brandhoek H 7a.1.3	01/11/1916	06/11/1916
War Diary	Ypres	06/11/1916	08/11/1916
War Diary	Right Sector	09/11/1916	10/11/1916
War Diary	Ypres	11/11/1916	17/11/1916
War Diary	Kaaie	18/11/1916	25/11/1916
War Diary	Brandhoek	26/11/1916	30/11/1916
Heading	War Diary Of The 164th Machine Gun Company For The Period 1st December To 31st December 1916 Vol XI		
Heading	War Diary Of This Company For The Month Of December 1916		
War Diary	Brandhoek	01/12/1916	07/12/1916
War Diary	Ypres	07/12/1916	17/12/1916
War Diary	Kaaie	18/12/1916	27/12/1916
War Diary	Brandhoek	28/12/1916	31/12/1916
Heading	War Diary Of The 164th M.G. Coy For The Period 1/1/17 To 31/1/17 Vol 12		
War Diary	Brandhoek	01/01/1917	06/01/1917
War Diary	Ypres Rt. Bde Sector	06/01/1917	10/01/1917
War Diary	Ypres	11/01/1917	23/01/1917
War Diary	S Camp	24/01/1917	31/01/1917
Heading	War Diary Of 164th Machine Gun Coy Feb 1917 Vol 13		
War Diary	S Camp	01/02/1917	04/02/1917
War Diary	Bollezeele	05/02/1917	16/02/1917
War Diary	Brandhoek	17/02/1917	25/02/1917
War Diary	Left Brigade Sector	26/02/1917	28/02/1917
Heading	War Diary 164th Machine Gun Company March 1917 Vol 14		
War Diary	Kaie Left Bde Sector	01/03/1917	16/03/1917
War Diary	Brandhoek	17/03/1917	27/03/1917
War Diary	Left Sector	28/03/1917	31/03/1917
Heading	War Diary Of 164th Machine Gun Company April 1917 Vol 15		
War Diary	Left Brigade Sector	01/04/1917	16/04/1917
War Diary	L Camp	17/04/1917	17/04/1917
War Diary	Houtkerque	18/04/1917	22/04/1917
War Diary	Noordpeene	23/04/1917	23/04/1917
War Diary	Hellebroucq	24/04/1917	30/04/1917
Heading	164th Machine Gun Company War Diary May 1917 Vol 16		
War Diary	Hellebroucq	01/05/1917	05/05/1917
War Diary	Noordpeene	06/05/1917	06/05/1917
War Diary	Brandhoek	07/05/1917	07/05/1917
War Diary	Left Bde Sector	08/05/1917	31/05/1917
Heading	164th Machine Gun Company War Diary For The Month Of June. Vol 17		
War Diary	Left Bde Sector	01/06/1917	11/06/1917
War Diary	Bollezeele	12/06/1917	15/06/1917
War Diary	Zutove	16/06/1917	30/06/1917

Heading	164th Machine Gun Company. War Diary For The Month Of July 1917 Vol 18		
War Diary	Brandhoek	01/07/1917	04/07/1917
War Diary	Left Sector	05/07/1917	09/07/1917
War Diary	Wieltje Sector	09/07/1917	20/07/1917
War Diary	Derby Camp	20/07/1917	23/07/1917
War Diary	Reay Camp	24/07/1917	25/07/1917
War Diary	Query Camp	26/07/1917	30/07/1917
War Diary	Divnl Sector	31/07/1917	31/07/1917
Operation(al) Order(s)	164th Machine Gun Company Order No. 126	26/07/1917	26/07/1917
Heading	War Diary Of 164th Machine Gun Coy August 1917 Vol 19		
War Diary	In The Line	31/07/1917	31/07/1917
War Diary	Divnl Sector	31/07/1917	06/08/1917
War Diary	Auden Fort	07/08/1917	31/08/1917
Heading	164th M.G. Coy War Diary For The Month Of September 1917 30 Sep 1917 Vol 20		
War Diary	Audenfort	01/09/1917	14/09/1917
War Diary	Goldfish Chateau (Ypres North Area)	15/09/1917	17/09/1917
War Diary	Wieltje	17/09/1917	24/09/1917
War Diary	Vlamertinghe	24/09/1917	24/09/1917
War Diary	Watou Area	24/09/1917	25/09/1917
War Diary	Bapaume	26/09/1917	26/09/1917
War Diary	Lechelle	27/09/1917	30/09/1917
Map	Position Of Guns		
Miscellaneous	Message Form		
Map	Positions Of Guns		
Miscellaneous	Message Form		
Map	Positions Of Guns		
Miscellaneous	Message Form		
Miscellaneous	164th Machine Gun Company.	18/09/1917	18/09/1917
Miscellaneous	Appendix II 164th Machine Gun Company.		
Heading	War Diary 164 M.G. Coy Oct 1917 Vol 21		
War Diary	Lechelle	01/10/1917	03/10/1917
War Diary	Aizecourt Le Bas	03/10/1917	11/10/1917
War Diary	Lempire Sector	12/10/1917	31/10/1917
Heading	War Diary For November 1917 164 M. Gun Coy. Vol 22		
War Diary	Lempire Sub. Sector	01/11/1917	01/11/1917
War Diary	Tincourt	02/11/1917	16/11/1917
War Diary	Lempire Sub. Sector	17/11/1917	23/11/1917
War Diary	Tincourt	24/11/1917	30/11/1917
War Diary	Lempire Sub Sector	30/11/1917	30/11/1917
Miscellaneous	164th Machine Gun Company Preliminary Order	17/11/1917	17/11/1917
Operation(al) Order(s)	164th Machine Gun Company Order No. 2	19/11/1917	19/11/1917
Heading	War Diary For December 1917 164th M. Gun Coy Vol 23		
War Diary	Epehy Sector	01/12/1917	02/12/1917
War Diary	Hamel	03/12/1917	04/12/1917
War Diary	Epehy Sector	04/12/1917	04/12/1917
War Diary	Villers Faucon	05/12/1917	05/12/1917
War Diary	Epehy Sector	06/12/1917	06/12/1917
War Diary	Hamel	06/12/1917	06/12/1917
War Diary	Flamicourt	07/12/1917	08/12/1917
War Diary	Habarcq	09/12/1917	13/12/1917
War Diary	Capelle Sur La Lys.	14/12/1917	31/01/1918

Heading	War Diary For February 1918 164th M. Gun Coy		
War Diary	Capelle Sur La Lys	01/02/1918	06/02/1918
War Diary	Enquin Les Mines	07/02/1918	07/02/1918
War Diary	Le Hamel	08/02/1918	08/02/1918
War Diary	Drouvin	09/02/1918	15/02/1918
War Diary	Canal Sector	15/02/1918	28/02/1918

4095/2924 (2)

4095/2924 (1)

55TH DIVISION
164TH INFY BDE

164TH MACHINE GUN COY.
FEB 1916-FEB 1918

O/c. Machine Gun Records.　　　1/3/16.
　　G.H.Q.
　　　　3rd Echelon.

Herewith confidential war diary of this
Coy, for month of February 1916.

　　　　　　　　　D. Pepplin. Capt.
　　　　　O.C. 164th Inf Bgde M.G. Coy

WAR DIARY or INTELLIGENCE SUMMARY

Army Form C. 2118.

Place	Date	Hour	Summary of Events and Information	Remarks and references to Appendices
SAULTY	19-2-16	Noon	The Company is officially recognised as part of the Pioneer Fm. Corps & is made up from Lewis Gun Sects. taken from the 164th & 165th Bgds:- namely, 1/4 Kings Own R.L. Rgt, 1/8 (Irish) Bn. K.L. Rgt, 1/4 Loyal North Lancs Fus, 2/5 Lancs Fus.	
Do.	19-2-16		Company Route March to SOMBRIN.	
	20-2-16	9 a.m.	O.C. inspection of billets & transport. Musketry instruction. Line of defence at WILLIET BASSUX.	
Do		9 a.m.	Senior Officers visit intermediate Line of defence at WILLIET BASSUX.	
Do	21-2-16	Noon	Company parade	
		8/H	Company parade	
Do	22-2-16	Noon	Company parade	
Do	23-2-16	Noon	Company parade	
	24-2-16	Noon	Company parade	
LE FERMONT	25-2-16	11am	Company leaves SAULTY & marches to LE FERMONT via MONCHIET. Coy. billeted 9 hundred at the village. No 3 Sect. proceeded at 5 p.m. with 1/4 L.N. Lancs Regt to Trenches to relieve 166 Brigade; remainder billet at LE FERMONT; transport returns to MONCHIET.	
Do.	26-2-16		No 2 Sect. proceeded with 1/4 R Lanc Regt to trenches to relieve B. 165 Brigade.	

Army Form C. 2118.

WAR DIARY
INTELLIGENCE SUMMARY.
(Erase heading not required.)

Instructions regarding War Diaries and Intelligence Summaries are contained in F. S. Regs., Part II. and the Staff Manual respectively. Title pages will be prepared in manuscript.

Place	Date	Hour	Summary of Events and Information	Remarks and references to Appendices
LA FERMONT	27-2-16		Nos 1 & 3 Sects in trenches, position for defence of BRETANCOURT chosen, indirect fire positions chosen.	
do	28-2-16		No 1 & 3 Sects in trenches, work on village defences started, allowance and placements for two 5" hows	
do	29-2-16		No 1 & 3 Sects in trenches, working parties from 7th Lanc two work on emplacement for village defences. — Indirect fire position at R.27.a.78.79 (Ref Map FIENEUX 1/10000 sh) is done.	

55

164 M G Cop
Vol II

WAR DIARY or INTELLIGENCE SUMMARY.

Army Form C. 2118.

16y Brig. Mach. Gun. Company

Place	Date	Hour	Summary of Events and Information	Remarks and references to Appendices
Fenwick	1/3/16		Nos 1 + 3 Sections in trenches: Work on indirect fire position No 2 Section	7pm.
	2/3/16		Nos 2+4 " relieve Nos 1+3 in trenches	8am
	3/3/16		Nos 2+4 Section in trenches: No 1 Section working on indirect fire position	9am
	4/3/16		" " " " : No 3 Section working on indirect fire position	7pm
	5/3/16		" " " " : indirect fire by Nos 1+3 on X30 67 + R34 D central	9pm 1250 rds fired
	6/3/16		" " " " : indirect fire on R35 C85,25 + R34 D central	9pm 1250 rds fired
	7/3/16		" " " " : indirect fire by Nos 1 + 3 on X3D 46	9pm 600 rds
	8/3/16		Nos 1+3 Section relieve Nos 2+4 : indirect fire by No 2+4 on X3D 9590	9pm 500 rds
	9/3/16		Nos 1+3 Section in trenches : indirect fire on and nw FISHEUX MILL	9pm 450 rds
	10/3/16		" " " " " : indirect fire on FISHEUX MILL	9pm 1250 rds
	11/3/16		" " " " " : indirect fire on R34 C.34	9pm 850 rds
	12/3/16		" " " " " : indirect fire on R34 B.63	9pm 1500 rds
	13/3/16		Nos 2+4 relieve Nos 1+3 in front line	
	14/3/16		Nos 2 + 4 Sections in trenches : indirect fire in conjunction with artillery on enemy transport on BLAIREVILLE - FICHEUX ROAD	7pm 500 rds
	15/3/16		" " " " "	
	16/3/16		" " " " " : indirect fire on N.W. corner of BLAIREVILLE WOOD	7pm 500 rds

Army Form C. 2118.

WAR DIARY
or
INTELLIGENCE SUMMARY.
(Erase heading not required.)

Instructions regarding War Diaries and Intelligence Summaries are contained in F.S. Regs., Part II. and the Staff Manual respectively. Title pages will be prepared in manuscript.

Place	Date	Hour	Summary of Events and Information	Remarks and references to Appendices
Fermont	17/3/16		Nos 2 & 4 Sections in front line: indirect fire on M.G. emns at BLAIREVILLE WOOD when 3500 rds. trenches were bombarded: also on R30C65,15; X3d67. 7TH	3500 rds.
"	18/3/16		Nos 2 & 4 in trenches: indirect fire on X3d67; R36A12,85, X4B35,85. 7TH	5000 rds.
"	19/3/16		" " " " : indirect fire on XSa21. 7TH	750 rds.
"	20/3/16		" " " " : indirect fire on sunken BLAIREVILLE-FICHEUX Road 5TH	5750 rds.
"	21/3/16		No 1 & 3 relieve No 2 & 4. 5TH	
"	22/3/16		No 1 & 3 Section in trenches.	
"	23/3/16		" " " " : No 4 sect moved into billet in BRETENCOURT. 5TH	
"	24/3/16		" " " " : No 2 Section " " " " " 5TH	
"	25/3/16		" " " " : between working party located & dispersed opposite Monte BLAIRE 5TH	
"	26/3/16		" " " " : No 1 Section exactly fresh emplacements in front line and house. 5TH	500 rds.
"	27/3/16		No 2 & 4 relieve No 1 & 3: indirect fire on X4C09. 5TH	JHH
"	28/3/16		No 2 & 4 in front line: much work appear to have been done on enemy lines at "the three trees" and X2d85. 5TH	JHH
"	29/3/16		" " " " : work on new emplacements. 5TH	JHH
"	30/3/16		" " " " : new emplacement completed in front line both machine guns 5TH	JHH
"	31/3/16		" " " " : allied plane brought down by enemy was down at R34d66. 5TH	JHH
			indirect fire on X3D69 5TH 800 rds.	

55

164 Bde M.G. Coy

Vol III

APRIL 1916. 164th Inf Bgde
Machine Gun Coy.

Army Form C. 2118.

WAR DIARY
or
INTELLIGENCE SUMMARY.
(Erase heading not required.)

Instructions regarding War Diaries and Intelligence Summaries are contained in F. S. Regs., Part II. and the Staff Manual respectively. Title pages will be prepared in manuscript.

Place	Date	Hour	Summary of Events and Information	Remarks and references to Appendices
Fonquevillers			MAP REFERENCES:- French Maps. EICHEUX 57c S.E. + 51b S.W. (Parts of)	
	1/4/16		Nos 2 & 4 Sections in trenches: Considerable aeroplane activity; red flares shown on the right	JFH
	2/4/16		" " " " : enemy transport train very distinct on the right: no trench mortar activity.	JFH
	3/4/16		Nos 1 & 3 relieve Nos 2 & 4 Sections: a Taub was distinctly heard in BLAIREVILLE at 7:30 am	JFH
	4/4/16		No 1 & 3 Sections in Trenches: Indirect fire was carried out on trays at X3 & 69; enemy working part at BRETENCOURT 6200 yds wire fires	JFH
	5/4/16		" " " " : Lights to the left of BLAIREVILLE WOOD	JFH
	6/4/16		" " " " : indirect fire on X3 B10.70; X4 a 46.50; X4 a 60.97	JFH 1250 "
	7/4/16		" " " " : indirect fire on R36 c 10.95; R35 a 50.15	JFH 3250 "
	8/4/16		" " " " : enemy machine gun most active; continued all night	JFH Central Division
	9/4/16		No 1 & 3 Sections in trenches, indirect fire on X5 13 X 59 Searching ground, 500 ms fire in enemy Sep Sn § 2030 am X3 B10.70 + BLAIREVILLE WOOD	
	10/4/16		No 1 v 3 Sec in trenches. Enemy M.G active at R35 a 45 80; Enemy working party fire on X3 B10.70	750 rounds
	11/4/16		No 1 v 3 Sec in trenches. 270 rounds fire at Enemy bumper at R34 C60 43. 300 rounds at R34 289 00	570 "
	12/4/16		No 2 & 4 Sect relieve No 1 v 3 ; Grand searches on X3 d. disperses rest work, indirect fire w.	JFH
			flaming targets from 3.15 pm - 7.15 pm R35a 40.70. R35 (37 41 X5 A 84 90 X5 A 20.10 Enemy replies with larger shells which failed to delur M.G.	2300 rounds
	13.4.16		No 2 v 4 Sect in trenches. Indirect fire in O.P. X3 B + Communication trench N.W. corner of BLAIREVILLE WOOD	6965 "

APRIL 1916. 164th Inf. Bgde.
Machine Gun Coy.

Army Form C. 2118.

WAR DIARY or INTELLIGENCE SUMMARY

(Erase heading not required.)

MAP REFERENCES — French Map
FICHEUX 51C S.E & 51B S.W (Parts of)

Place	Date	Hour	Summary of Events and Information	Remarks and references to Appendices
La Herrmont	14/4/16		Nos 2 & 4 Secs. in trenches. Heavier transport than usual heard on FICHEUX-BLAIREVILLE ROAD	Rd 1050 rds
"	15/4/16		Points fires on R34 b45 43. R34 c45.40	" 720 "
"	16/4/16		Working party at R34 b 8 9. fired on.	
"			Between 9 p.m. & 12.30 p.m. Enemy sent up a number of flares. Two sets fired by M.Gs whilst flares. Flash of enemy battery observed at 11.45 p.m. & X4 80.30.	
"			Loudest fire with M.Gs on ground east of enemy support line at R35.A from 7.45 p.m. – 10.30 p.m.	3550 "
"	17/4/16		Loudest fire in centre nt. with rain guns on X4 80.35, X4 80.35 from 12.15 a.m. – 3.40 a.m. This fire rendered great assistance to working party	8300 "
"	18/4/16		Cutting enemy wire. Indirect fire on X4 A80.75. X4 80.85 from 12.45 am – 2.50 am Zero. Working party No 2 left front on Sap R34 C90.55. 7 Perriers in work	" 8800 "
"	19/4/16		Nos 1 & 3 recd. relieve Nos 2 & 4. M.Gs fire on points R34 C38.50 – R34 C 52.90.	" 1040 "
"	20/4/16		" M.G. fire on trenches & when working party worked	" 870 "
"	21/4/16		R35.A3.5 fires on & R33 30.55	" 420 "
"	22/4/16		Enemy very quiet. M.G. traverses enemy parapet & wire where at his own end	" 330 "
"	23/4/16		" "	" 630 "

APRIL 1916 164' Inf Bde
Machine Gun Coy.

Army Form C. 2118

WAR DIARY
or
INTELLIGENCE SUMMARY

(Erase heading not required.)

Instructions regarding War Diaries and Intelligence Summaries are contained in F.S. Regs., Part II. and the Staff Manual respectively. Title Pages will be prepared in manuscript.

MAP REFERENCES – Trench Map
FICHEUX 51C SE + 51C SW (Part 1)

Place	Date	Hour	Summary of Events and Information	Remarks and references to Appendices
Bellacourt	24/4/16		No 1 + 3 Sects in trenches. Enemy's working parties dispersed by M.G. where were hostile out by raiding party. R34 b.9.75 fired on by No 3.	TSU 1180 rd
"	25/4/16		No " " " " No 2 Sect. relieved 166' Bgde. R34 b.28.12 our artillery out. Enemy active. M. Gun fired on the front during the night at intervals	TSU 930 "
			Stg – hrs	
"	26/4/16		No 3 Sect relieved by No 4. No 2 sect with 166 Bgde. Increased rifle + M.G. fire by enemy between 7.30 + midnight. Enemy M.G. fired fire from point X3.6.8.9 at 8.30 p.m. two of our guns retaliated immediately. Enemy M. Gun did not fire again during the night. Indirect fire was carried out in points R36.A.1.8 + R36.A.3.5. between 9 p.m. + 10 p.m. 1500 rounds fired	TSU 2850 rds
"	27/4/16		No 1 + 4 Sections in trenches. No 2 sect with 166' Bgde. Enemy's working party fired on at point X3.6.10.75. Enemy's parapet swept at intervals in front of BLAIREVILLE WOOD	TSU 1800 rds
"	28/4/16		No 1 + 4 sections in trenches. No 2 sect with 166' Bgde. Curious craters BLAIREVILLE WOOD at intervals	TSU 230 rds
"	29/4/16		No 1 + 4 " " " No 2 " " " " Enemy working party dispersed at R 34 C.2.3. Indirect fire on point R35.a.80.05. at 8 p.m – 9 p.m	TSU 1750 rds
"	30/4/16		No 1 section relieved by No 3 sect. No 4 Sect in trenches. No 2 Sect with 166' Bgde. Indirect fire in front R35.a.80.05 at 3 – 4 AM.	TSU 1000 rds

1875 Wt. W593/826 1,000,000 4/15 J.B.C. & A. A.D.S.S./Forms/C. 2118.

Army Form C. 2118

WAR DIARY
or
INTELLIGENCE SUMMARY
(Erase heading not required.)

164 Inf. Bgde. Machine Gun Co.

Instructions regarding War Diaries and Intelligence Summaries are contained in F.S. Regs., Part II. and the Staff Manual respectively. Title Pages will be prepared in manuscript. **MAP REFERENCES**

Place	Date	Hour	Summary of Events and Information	Remarks and references to Appendices
LE FERMONT	1/5/16		TRENCH MAP: FICHEUX. 51C S.E. & 51 B S.W. (Parts of). No 2 Section relief Right Sub Sector. No 2 Sect with 166' Bgde. No 4 Sect in Left Sub Sector. 300 rounds fired at R.33. D.9.3. 100 rounds at R.34. B.8.8.	T.M. 400 rds
"	2/5/16		No 3 & 4 Sections in trenches. No 2 Sect with 166' Bgde: Indirect fire was carried out on the following targets R.33. B.10.40. R.36. Q.1.8. – R.36. Q.10.15. 5 – 6 p.m. R.35 c. 2.3. R.35 a. 1.4. R.33. B.10.40. 10.30 – 11.30 p.m. 750 rds. 1000 rds. Snipers nests being made in the fields 750 rounds	T.M. 2500 rds
"	3/5/16		No 3 & 4 Sections in trenches. No 2 Sect with 166' Bgde. BLAIREVILLE WOOD traversed at intervals during day & night. Teams working on new emplacements & putting in Emplacement Boards.	T.M. 2100 rds
"	4/5/16		No 1 Sect. relieved No 4: No 3 Sect. in trenches. No 2 with 166' Bgde. Indirect fire on R.35 c.23 & FICHEUX MILL. 1000 rds. 1250 rounds R.34 C.17.28. BLAIREVILLE WOOD	T.M. 2500 rds
"	5/5/16		No 1 Sect. relieved No 4 in trenches. No 3 Sect in trenches. No 2 with 166' Bgde. Intermittent machine gun fire from MONCHIET to SIMENCOURT. BLAIREVILLE WOOD traversed at intervals	T.M. 940 rds
"	6/5/16	11 AM	No 1 & 3 in trenches. No 2 Sect with 166' Bgde. Indirect fire on X.3.C.5.5 & X.3.D.60.20 when fire was opened on X.3.C.5.5 Enemy replied with 4 light Shrapnel. Enemy's front line & BLAIREVILLE WOOD fired on during the 24 hours.	T.M. 1300 rds
"	7/5/16	6.30 p.m.	No 1 & 3 Sect in trenches. No 2 Sect with 166' Bgde. Enemy machine guns fired from front R.34 C.5.7 at 6.30 p.m. One of our guns replied. Enemy did not fire again. Indirect fire on X.3.D.6.4. X.4 B.35.85. R.35 A.2.3. when firing in the latter point shots were heard by our sentry in the front line.	T.M. 3250

1875 Wt. W.593/826 1,000,000 4/15 J.B.C. & A. A.D.S.S./Forms/C. 2118.

Army Form C. 2118

WAR DIARY
or
INTELLIGENCE SUMMARY 164th Inf. Bde.
Machine Gun Coy.

(Erase heading not required.)

Instructions regarding War Diaries and Intelligence Summaries are contained in F.S. Regs., Part II. and the Staff Manual respectively. Title Pages will be prepared in manuscript.

MAP REFERENCES
FICHEUX
51 C. S.E. & 51 B. S.W.

Place	Date	Hour	Summary of Events and Information	Remarks and references to Appendices
In Trenches	8/5/16		9°1 & 3 Sections N°2 with 166th Bgde: Indirect fire on R.35.a.2.3. Enemy working on R.44.a.44.65	Diff. 182 rds
"	9/5/16		" " " 700 rounds fired on the front Indirect fire from 8.30-10pm. Enemy rifles with Lewis G	3800 "
"	10/5/16		" 1.&4 " " " Shrapnel. BLAIREVILLE WOOD was reported that the day sweept Enemy machine gun active about K.3.a.95.20	Fired 890 "
"	11/5/16		" 1.&4 " " N° 2 rifles from 166th BLAIREVILLE WOOD. Occasional searching fire enemy working party dispersed at K.2.b.12	390 "
"	12/5/16		" 1.&4 " " Enemy very inactive. BLAIREVILLE WOOD searched	400 "
"	13/5/16		" 1.&4 " " Indirect fire on enemy wire where it had been cut by artillery	2130 "
"	14/5/16		" 1.&4 " " N°3 relieved 165th Bgde by Gun Coy. BLAIREVILLE WOOD searched	440 "
"	15/5/16		" 1.&4 " " N°3 with 165th Bgde. Indirect fire from 9pm-4am.	2050 "
"	16/5/16		" 2.&4 " " Enemy machine guns active. Indirect fire from 9-11.30pm	1730 "
"	17/5/16		" 2.&4 " " BLAIREVILLE WOOD searched. Enemy working parties more active. These were fired upon.	1600 "
"	18/5/16		" 2.&4 " " Indirect fire 11.pm-midnight Enemy aeroplanes dropped range n° parachutes X.1.b.3.8. Enemy transport heard at 9pm. Harrier 11in mount. OSIER BEDS kept under fire at intervals. Indirect fire at 7pm. BLAIREVILLE	1730 "
"	19/5/16		" 2.&4 " " WOOD searched. Indirect fire 8-12 midnight. Enemy's parapet knocked down. 2 knocked - Indirect fire	2150 "
"	20/5/16		" 2.&1 " " " " 3.30 - 11.30pm	3350 "

T. J. E. Willoughby Lieut.
O.C. 164 Bgde

WAR DIARY
or
INTELLIGENCE SUMMARY

(Erase heading not required.) 1/6th Sea. Bn. Black Watch (T.F.)

Army Form C. 2118

Place	Date	Hour	Summary of Events and Information	Remarks and references to Appendices
La Hermitte	21/5/16		No 2 & 1 sections in trenches 40.3 sect with 165. Bgde. Enemy putting up new wire R2W. S 65.45 - 65.60	
"	22/5/16	"	BLAIREVILLE WOOD Trenched. Intermit fire 9 - 11.30pm	To 2650
"	23/5/16	"	" " " 7 - 10.30pm Enemy sniper with light shrapnel incid fire 3.5pm - 4pm	To 2650
"	24/5/16	4 · 1	BLAIREVILLE WOOD shelled intermit fire 4 - 6pm	To 4750
"	25/5/16	4 · 1	3 - 7pm 8 - 10.30pm 9 - 10pm Enemy light guns more active, enfilade searching of machine guns. BLAIREVILLE WOOD shelled. Gadmur fire 8 - 9pm 4pm-4.45pm 10-10.45. 10.30-11.30pm 7am, 8am 3 - 3.45pm	To 5350
"	26/5/16	"	BLAIREVILLE WOOD trenched. Intermit fire 8pm-11.30pm 3am. 3.30am	To 2050
"	27/5/16	"	BLAIREVILLE WOOD shelled. Working party fired on. Enemy rifles with T.M. Intermit fire 8.30pm - midnight	To 3550
"	28/5/16	2 + 4		
"	29/5/16	2 + 4	BLAIREVILLE WOOD was shelled from time to time during the day	To 3580

WAR DIARY
or
INTELLIGENCE SUMMARY

(Erase heading not required.)

164th Ind Bgde Machine Gun Coy.

Army Form C. 2118

Place	Date	Hour	Summary of Events and Information	Remarks and references to Appendices
Jos. Bronfay	30/3/18		N° 2 & 4 actions in trenches. N°3 rest with 165th Bgde. Enemy shelled LIVERPOOL S&D between 11.30pm & 1am. The most pronounced on M Sap down in great strength. 2/Lt Hodler, No 2775 Pte Hollowell & No 3093 Pte Hargreaves behaved with great coolness. Subjected to heavy shell fire they remained at the gun, exposed to ammunition to the shelter. Their retirement moved in case which was blocked, the retreat being a question of duty seeing always against the line forward. The 164 Bgde 500 rds fired into HENDECOURT - BLAIREVILLE WOOD searches fire from 11.30 - dawn. Intermit. fire from 8-9 pm.	Ap. 2230
"	31/3/18		N° 2 & 4 rest in trenches. N° 3. with 165 Bgde — N°3 rest relieved by 165th Pn. G Coy. 9p-2.4. relieved by 166 M.G. Coy - Indirect fire on BLAIREVILLE WOOD Coy hqrs LEFERMONT at 10 pm. via BEAUMETZ - MONCHIET, arriving at GOUY at 12.10 midnight.	Ap. 1375

J.B.S. Welly
Lieut
O.C. 164 M.G.

Army Form C. 2118

WAR DIARY
or
INTELLIGENCE SUMMARY
(Erase heading not required.)

Instructions regarding War Diaries and Intelligence Summaries are contained in F.S. Regs., Part II. and the Staff Manual respectively. Title Pages will be prepared in manuscript.

Place	Date	Hour	Summary of Events and Information	Remarks and references to Appendices
Gouy in Artois	1/6/16		Map Reference 51.C + 51.B S.W. 1	
	1/6/16 to 18/6/16		Company left LEFERMONT at 10.30 pm 31/5/16 arrived in GOUY at midnight	
	18/6/16		Company training in Gouy. Tactical schemes inspected by Major General H.S. Jeudwine. Company moves from Gouy at 1.45 pm via SIMENCOURT BERNEVILLE WALRUS	
			DAINEVILLE. Relieve the 43rd Bgde M. Guns Co in G Sector. Relief completed by 2.45 am 19/6/16. No 3 Section in village AGNY – No 2 Front Line. No 1. Right Support. No 4 Left Support TRANSPORT at WALRUS	
DAINEVILLE	19/6/16		All Sections in trenches. Enemy quiet.	
	20/6/16		All Sections in trenches. Situation normal.	
	21/6/16		" " "	
	22/6/16		" " " Transport moved to SIMENCOURT	
	23/6/16		" " " many trench mortars active	
	24/6/16		" " "	
	25/6/16		" " " Enemy trench mortars rifle grenades active. Our emplacements damaged	
	26/6/16		Gun posts knocked out. Batteries. All Sections in trenches. Situation normal. Great activity shown by our artillery	

Army Form C. 2118

WAR DIARY
or
INTELLIGENCE SUMMARY

(Erase heading not required.) 164" Machine Gun Coy.

Place	Date	Hour	Summary of Events and Information	Remarks and references to Appendices
DAINEVILLE	27/6/16	MAP. REF. 51B S.W.	Enemy trench mortars very active, but trench mortars replied effectively & did much damage to enemy wire to advanced work at M.20.a N.E. Between 3pm & 4pm 2500 rounds were fired hit BEAURAINES. Flanking fire & Cover fire attack delivered by 141st Divn 43 Bgde.	T.S.O.
"	28/6/16		Enemy comparatively quiet - during the night, judging by the numbers of flares sent up. The enemy in a "jumpy" condition.	T.S.O.
"	29/6/16	At 5pm. heavy bombardment on night by our artillery. The enemy's lines at 3.30-5.30 A.M. Enemy bombarded heavily from 3.15 - 5 pm. Shells put into N.E. end of DAINEVILLE - Little damage done - Enemy Trench mortars again very active -	T.S.O.
"	30/6/16		Fairly quiet - Our artillery very active - Enemy transport heard between 10.30pm & midnight	T.S.O.

164th Brigade.

55th Division.

164th BRIGADE.

MACHINE GUN COMPANY

JULY 1 9 1 6

Vol 5

War Diary
of the
164th Inf. Bde. Machine Gun Company,
55th (West Lancashire) Division
for the period
1st July, 1916 to 31st July 1916.

WAR DIARY or INTELLIGENCE SUMMARY

Army Form C. 2118

(Erase heading not required.)

Place	Date	Hour	Summary of Events and Information	Remarks and references to Appendices
DAINEVILLE	1/7/16		Company in trenches in G. Sector. Reference map NEUVILLE VITASSE. Relieved in the night 12/7/13 by 166th Manch. Regt. & 29.	JSU
	12/7/16			JSU
BARLY.	12/7/16		Company at BARLY. Training - No 3 Section in trenches E Sector Ref. Map FICHEUX	JSU
	20/7/16		Company marched to IVERGNY at 7.15 am via SOMBRIN Sus ST LEDGER arriving at 11 am. Guide Rfl. LENS II	JSU
	20/7/16		" left IVERGNY at 7.15 am & marched to GEZAINCOURT via LE SOUICH, BOUQUMAISON HEM - arriving at 11.15 am. Map ref. LENS II.	JSU
	21/7/16		Company marched to BERNEUL at 7.15 am via LONGUEVILLETTE, FIENVILLERS arriving at 12 noon. Ref Map. LENS II	JSU
	22/7/16		Resting at BERNEUL	JSU
	23/7/16		TRANSPORT left BERNEUL at 8 am. for RAINNEVILLE via CANAPLES, HAVERNAS, FLESSELLES, VILLERS BOCAGE arriving at 1.30 pm.	JSU
	24/7/16		Company interned at CANDAS arrived at MERICOURT 11.30 am then marched to MEAULTE Map Ref 62 D N.E - Transport left RAINNEVILLE 6 am via ALLONVILLE QUERRIEU, HEILLY, RIBEMONT, TREUX MEAULTE, arriving at 2 pm.	JSU
	25/7/16			JSU
	26/7/16		Company marched to L 3 A (HAPPY VALLEY) at 4 pm. Ref 62 D	JSU
	27/7/16		" in camp at HAPPY VALLEY.	JSU

WAR DIARY or INTELLIGENCE SUMMARY

Army Form C. 2118

Place	Date	Hour	Summary of Events and Information	Remarks and references to Appendices
	28/7/16		Company in Camp - HAPPY VALLEY	
	29/7/16		" " " HAPPY VALLEY	
	30/7/16		Nº1 & Nº2 Sections left HAPPY VALLEY. Map Ref. 62D N.E. L3A at 7.30 pm and marched to trenches relieving Nº 93rd M.G.Coy at 5.30 pm on 31st inst. Map Ref. GUILLEMONT A6. Nº3 & 4 Sections left HAPPY VALLEY at 10.40 pm & marched to CASEMENT TRENCH. A10 B. TRANSPORT returned to camp near BRONFAY FARM	
NEAR TRONES WOOD	31/7/16		Nº 1 & 2 Sections in Trenches Enemy shelled trenches & supports heavily during day & night. 1 man killed Nº 1 Sect. Pte ATKINSON 2 men Nº 1 Sect. wounded. 1 Shell shock (Cpl McIntyre) Pte HALL Nº 4 Sect. killed - Pte GRADWELL Nº 2 Sect. wounded - Nº 4 Sect. in CASEMENT TRENCH. Nº 3 Sect. in BRIQUETERIE - Cpl GREEN Nº 4 Sect. wounded - Nº 3 Sect. relieved Nº 2 & Nº 4 relieved Nº 1.	
Dº	1/8/16			
	2/8/16			

Watson Capt.
Comdg 164 M.G. Coy.

164th Brigade.
55th Division.

164th BRIGADE. MACHINE GUN COMPANY

AUGUST 1 9 1 6

Account of operations attached:

Army Form C. 2118.

WAR DIARY
or
INTELLIGENCE SUMMARY. 164th Machine Gun Coy

(Erase heading not required.)

Place	Date	Hour	Summary of Events and Information	Remarks and references to Appendices
In trenches near TRONES WOOD	1/8/16		No 3 Sect. relieved No 2 Sect. No 2 returned to CASEMENT TRENCH	JSJ
			No 4 " No 1 " No 1 " BRIQUETERIE	JSJ
			Enemy Artillery active.	
	2/8/16		At 8.30pm a party of 1/4 Kings Own R.L. Regt. crossed the sunken road to Couquilhon with a party of 1/18 Kings Liv. with the objective of mending an enemy dugout at S.30.D (Guillemont Map). Enemy were there in force about 200. The STOKES TRENCH MORTAR opened first & the enemy's fires began to retire in disorder. Thereupon 2 guns of No 3 Sect & 2 guns of No 4 let enfilade traverse & then good target presented by the flying germans & inflicted severe losses. Enemy retaliated with 7 severe bombardment no casualties to the Machine Gun section.	JSJ
	3/8/16		Pte Lyons suffering with shell shock — No 1 Sect relieved by No 4. No 2 relieved No 3. 2nd Collier wounded from return of fire from pistol.	JSJ
	4/8/16		No 3 sect relieved by 165th M.G.Coy at 9 pm & returned to No 4 Sect. Ptn Levert No 4 Sect- wounded.	JSJ
	5/8/16		Transport. No 1 & 2 sect returned by 165th M.G.Coy & returned to BRIQUETERIE & Companion Men TRENCH.	JSJ

Army Form C. 2118.

WAR DIARY
or
INTELLIGENCE SUMMARY.
(Erase heading not required.)

104 Machine Gun Coy

Instructions regarding War Diaries and Intelligence Summaries are contained in F. S. Regs., Part II. and the Staff Manual respectively. Title pages will be prepared in manuscript.

Place	Date	Hour	Summary of Events and Information	Remarks and references to Appendices
In Trenches B:Graves Wood	6/8/16		Nos 3 & 4 Sections with Transport Nos 1 & 2 in Billets.	
	7/8/16		No 3 Sect. Left Transport at 6.30 a.m. & marched to join the Section No 4. Left at 8.30 p.m. mounted to join the Line Sections Nos 1 & 2 front line.	
Guillemont	8/8/16		At 4 a.m. in the morning 8th & 9th Hull Brigade attacked GUILLEMONT. No 2 Section 8th & 9th G Coy was ordered to get into position in trench west from between GINCHY & GUILLEMONT No 1 Gun & the other about 100x WNW they remain at 4.30 a.m. II Division advanced the guns almost made the jump. about 100x from GUILLEMONT STATION. During the event the two outposts, ENEMY M.G. and bombers after making 4 & 5 attacks on troops established themselves well the M.G. fire & bombs rifle fire. Our fourth attempt Cpl RAWTON took the gun forward with Cpl HOARE. The front was covered, the latter helped. Cpl RAWTON getting wounded when Gun & two teams forward to original position. The enemy shells heavily & guns are withdrawn to advance trench where it remained without loss about 4 pm. 17 Bombers sent in charge of Sergt of section of No 2 Section. Guns now are in the Sect. of Railway on left of 1/8 Liverpool Irish. Our troops were held up by M.G. Lewis rifle fire. No 3 Section under Lt Tinker was allotted to 1/6 King's Dugouts. Then action prior with 2nd wave of the attack & advanced 300x to German wire. Our troops were held up. Returned intact, no serious trouble. Targets were German in action of German troops running from GINCHY & GUILLEMONT. The section was relieved at 1 a.m. on 9/8/16	

1577 Wt. W10791/1773 50,000 1/15 D. D. & L. A.D.S.S./Forms/C. 2118.

WAR DIARY or INTELLIGENCE SUMMARY

Army Form C. 2118.

164th Machine Gun Coy

Place	Date	Hour	Summary of Events and Information	Remarks and references to Appendices
GUILLEMONT	8/8/16		Under the charge of 2/Lt PURNELL No1 Sect was detailed to 1/4 Kings Own F.L. Regt'n. On arrival at Emery was heavy M.G. bomb rifle fire was encountered. The infantry retired. On recent attack was made but was again repulsed. 2/Lt McDIARMID in charge of B. M. left his sector rather the infantry for which attack which was again unsuccessful. 2/Lt McDIARMID was killed — When being received to the troops & retire to an advanced trench. No.4 Sect took up position to bring fire arms E from 8 GUILLEMONT. Capt SARTORIUS in charge. 2 left his Sec. 2/Lt HARTINGTON 8th night hey dent. Position taken up — Support trench — Gun took up position in shell hole in front. B. Col Sec were Enemy front heavy M.G. fire, bomb rifle fire. On retirement infantry M.G. retreat to rear. The M.G. Coy lost. McFISHER, 2/Lt McDIARMID killed. 17 wounded. Capt. D RALSTON Wounded O.R. killed 17 wounded. 2 guns lost.	
	8/8/16		M.G. Company arrived back at — TRANSPORT	
	9/8/16		Company resting near BONAFAY FARM	
	10/8/16		" " "	
	11/8/16		" " "	
	12/8/16		" " "	

Army Form C. 2118.

WAR DIARY
or
INTELLIGENCE SUMMARY.
(Erase heading not required.)

164th Machine Gun Coy

Instructions regarding War Diaries and Intelligence Summaries are contained in F. S. Regs., Part II. and the Staff Manual respectively. Title pages will be prepared in manuscript.

Place	Date	Hour	Summary of Events and Information	Remarks and references to Appendices
Park Bompas Farm	13/8/16		Company in Bivouac	
	14/8/16		" " Méricourt	
Méricourt	15/8/16		" " Méricourt	
"	16/8/16		" "	
"	17/8/16		" "	
"	18/8/16		Transport moved at 3.30 pm to Douens	
"	19/8/16		Company entrained at 6.15 am at Méricourt. Detrained at Cahon (Somme). 7 men into billets. Transport arrived at 9 pm.	
Cahon (Somme)	20/8/16 to 30/8/16		Company training at Cahon. On 28/8/16 Transport moved to Méricourt (Somme). Entrained at 7 am 30/8/16 at Pont Remy & Company marched from Cahon to Pont Remy where it entrained for Méricourt, arriving there at 11 am. Bivouac billets & Company into camp	
	31/8/16		moved to Albert - Amiens main road. Sends crews forward to road	

1577 Wt.W10791/1773 50,000 1/15 D.D.&L. A.D.S.S./Forms/C. 2118.

Operation Report of 164 M.G. Coy.
from 4 A.M. 8/8/16 to 9/8/16.

Company was split up into sections –
2 sections were allotted to 1/4 Kings Own
& 1/8 Liverpool Rgt.
One section was sent to guard left flank of attack
& one section to guard right flank –

No. 3 Section (Lt Fisher) was allotted to 1/8
Liverpool Irish, who sent 1 gun with each coy.
with orders to follow attack and make strong
points on E side of village.
at 11.0 P.M. 7/8/16 guns took position behind
advance trench. At 4.15 A.M 8/8/16
they advanced with 2nd line of attack. &
arrived at German Parapet – They were
then very heavily bombed with smoke & gas
bombs, and were forced to retire with infantry,
as far as own advanced trench – where positions
were taken up – Lt Fisher was missed at
this point, he was very gallantly leading his
men, & when held up, rallied some infantry
& led an attack on parapet – Subsequently,
2 M. Guns opened fire on 2 parties of 30 Germans,
crossing from GUILLEMONT to STATION
& accounted for a good percentage of them.
These Guns were relieved at 1. A.M. on 9/8/16 by
166 M.G. Coy. Casualties 10 O.R. missing 2 O.R. missing

2

and 7. O.R. wounded.

No. 4 Section was posted on Rt. flank with orders to take up final position at T25C47 to fire N.E. across front of final objective. Position was taken up in Support Trench at 1. A.M 8/8/16 – Guns advanced on right of Infantry at 3.50 A.M. On reaching point S30B5530 heavy M.G. fire was opened by enemy at about 4.15 A.M. from a point well within our Barrage. The enemy also threw many smoke & a few gas bombs – The Infantry attack was held up, & finally driven in – 2 left guns under Capt. Sartorius stayed in shell hole, and finally retired into adv. trench – a patrol crept forward to try & get fire onto Enemy guns, but were unable to do so — 3 guns (1 spare) under 2 Lt Hartington on being fired on passed off to Rt. into sunken road, and nearly reached enemy barricade, but were unprotected, and were forced to retire to own barricade – where they dug in — At 10.30 guns came under own artillery fire & had to retire — 3 men of other units wounded here (5)
2/Lt Hartington then organised right flank guns to completely cover ground as far as ARROW HEAD COPSE
Casualties. 1 O.R. Killed.
1 C.S.M. Killed.

3.

No. 1 Section (2/Lts Purnell & McDiarmid) was posted to 1/4 Kings Own — one gun to each coy, with orders to advance & make strong points E of village —

Rt. Guns took up positions in advanced trench (EDWARDS TRENCH) at 3.45 A.M. 8/8/16. at 3.50 A.M. guns advanced with 1st line — ~~On ad~~ After advancing 60ˣ ~~~~ uncut barbed wire was met, & enemy opened heavy M.G. fire & gas bombs (no smoke bombs) Orders were passed down (from the left) to retire slowly into advanced trench. where positions were taken up — Fire was opened to cover retirement of infantry. On infantry retiring ~~from front line and to~~ to avoid own artillery fire, the 2 rear guns remained to hold position. Relieved at 4. A.M. 9/8/16 — 2nd Lt Purnell suffering from shell shock returned at 8.P.M. 8/8/16.

Remaining 2 guns under 2/Lt McDiarmid advanced from N. of ARROW HEAD COPSE at 3.45 A.M. 8/8/16 and reached uncut enemy wire, where they were subjected to heavy M.G. fire & smoke & gas bombs. They retired with the Company to adv. trench. (with 1 gun hit in steam tube & out of action) 2 Lt Mc. Diarmid was seen collecting the some men of the infantry and leading an attack on the enemies wire, which was apparently unpassable

4

These guns then took up positions in trench N of ARROW HEAD COPSE.
Relieved at 4 A.M. 9/8/16
 Casualties   1 Of. missing
              1 Of. shell shock.
              1 OR. killed
              1 OR missing
              8 O.R. wounded.

No. 2 Section. (Lt. Brooke) took up positions in front of advance trench — at 11.30 p.m. 7/8/16 & dug in — ~~Behind Infantry Advanced~~.
2 guns under Lt Brooke were in position S of Railway — at 4.20 they advanced towards STATION behind 2nd Division, who arrived at STATION but were driven out again. guns reached 50ˣ from station, and retired with Infantry, & took up position in shell hole in front (20ˣ) of advanced trench, to cover front of Infantry. Advanced trench S of Railway was empty, for at least 400ˣ (from Railway to beyond TRONES GUILLEMONT ROAD). At 7 P.M. under cover of Artillery bombardment (own) these guns retired to trench S. 30 a 59 by order of O.C. Irish.
The remaining 2 guns under Capt. Ralston were N of Railway — They advanced with Infantry, but were held up about 100ˣ short of

STATION – Capt Ralston took one gun up
Railway, but was unable to get a target.
Shortly after, he was wounded and gun was
buried. Both guns retired to Advanced
Trench, where they took up positions until
relieved by guns of 7th Division at about
10 p.m.

Casualties – 1 Offr. wounded.
1 O.R. missing.
5 O.R. wounded.

On the whole.
Morale very good indeed.
Men worked well helping dig out
trenches as well as dig emplacements.
No good targets offered themselves.
A large no. of belt boxes lost in consequence
of heavy casualties in carrying parties.

L. Sartoris Capt.
Comdg. 164. M.G. Coy.

M.G. Left Section   1.
No. 2 Section.   No. 1 Gun.

Cpl Lumb was in charge of this gun
under Capt Ralston.

The gun had orders to finally get into
position in Z Z trench and sweep ground
between GINCHY and GUILLEMONT.
I arrived in an advance trench about 11 P.M.
7/8/16 and we dug ourselves in about 30ˣ
in front of advance trench on left of
Railway — At 4.20 A.M. II Division in front
of us advanced — at 4.30 AM. gun advanced
until level with own troops, who were lying
down & firing. about 100ˣ from station —
They seemed to be firing on a sap running out
from their enemy line towards the railway.
Owing to the mist it was hard to see — The
enemy were throwing smoke bombs. I did
not notice any gas or wire — After some
short time our troops retired, with some germans
prisoners (about 6) taken by an officer — after having
made 4 or 5 attacks, each time being held
up by M.G. fire bombs and rifle fire —
At fourth attack Capt. Ralston took my gun
with him out to front but got wounded.
L Cpl. O'Hara was taken prisoner or killed.
Capt. Ralston ordered my gun back — we
took gun back down Railway & then N.
into original place in advance of trench —
The enemy shelled us heavily after thour

2

in this position, so the gun was withdrawn into
advance trench, where we remained till
relieved about 9. p.m.
I think 1 German M.G. was firing from our
right front from high ground behind
GUILLEMONT.

L. Cpl. McMurray was with No. 2 gun on
the right of No. 1 gun. he states that
~~his gun~~ movements of his gun were similar
to those of No. 1. except that he did not
advance the second time —
The gun, tripod and ammunition with 2
men were buried — but dug out.
he has no remarks to make —

~~Lt. Simpson was with No. 3 gun.~~
Lt. Brooke was in charge of Rt ½ section
of No. 2. Section — he states.
We dug in in advance of front line about
100 S of Railway on left of Liverpool
Irish — 2nd Division ~~to~~ right was on
the railway. At 4.20 Infantry who
had already crawled out 100˟ in advance
of trench attacked. at 4.25 a number
of ~~all~~ infantry came rushing back, saying
they had been ordered to retire — a Sgt.
of N. Lancs (Sgt. Hill) said he had ordered
his men to retire (He was in charge of
a platoon of the carrying party of N. Lancs)

because both his men and the attacking party (Irish) had been held up by M.G. fire.
An Offr from II Divn came in wounded saying that his men had reached G. 1st line trench, & were digging in a few yards on the other side. His was the left Btn. of the IInd Divn. He said that the Rt. Btn. (Middlesex) had been held up —
Capt Ralston also arrived & ordered us to stand fast — We went together up to GUILLEMONT & TRONES Road to see what was happening. The N. Lancs were still coming back. (This was about 4.45 A.M.) We returned to the guns. Capt Ralston again went off to the Right (GUILLEMONT RD) & on returning said 'The Trench Mortars are going over'.
My 2 guns then started towards the STATION After moving some 100ᵃ Capt RALSTON ordered us to come back, as infantry on left of Railway were retiring — We retired into a shell hole ~~~~ in front of Advanced Trench — which was empty — At 8¾ p.m. we retired under cover of smoke from own bombardment into trench next to TRONES WOOD under orders from O.C. Irish.
I heard from some men of North Lancs who had retired, that Left Company of Kings had been forced back, & that the Germans had ~~~~ got in behind the Irish through

4

the gap so formed & had so cut them
off — Our lewis guns ~~and Guns~~
were in action in direction of village.
& there was much M.G. Fire (German)
from Rt. & left of village. About 5° or 5.15 A.M.
there was a heavy mist on all the time —

L. Cpl. Dolan. No 4 gun. says he thinks
German M.G. was on high ground
N. of ARROW HEAD COPSE. (strong
point?)
Pte. Simpson ~~says~~ No 3 gun. says.
Whole advance ~~of~~ up valley was commanded
from this high ground.
At about 8 or 9 A.M. No 3 gun saw
a party of about 10 four men carrying a gun
retiring from high ground near ARROW HD.
COPSE —

Sgt. Griffin (with Rt. ½ section) says.
M.G. fire (German) appeared to be from
strong point N. of ARROW HEAD COPSE
and from direction of GINCHY RIDGE.
Range ~~probably~~ of latter probably 800-1000ˣ.
At about 9.20 A.M. Pte. Welsh (Irish) came
in front, & said there were 8 men of 1st Kings
& about 12 Irish dug in at STATION.
They were surrounded — He slipped away at
dusk —

No. 3. Section.   6
   Allotted to Liverpool Irish.
Commander Lt Fisher.

   Left half Section.
Sgt. Collinson states —
The orders given to my half section were
to bear to the left of the village, and
make strong point on N.E. of village.
We took up position behind front
line of Irish near their left flank.
At about 4.15 am. Irish advanced.
We had orders to proceed with 2nd
line of attack. but these bore to their
right & left my guns in the air.
The carrying party of N. Lancs ~~however~~
who were behind 2nd line of attack
bore to their left towards the quarry.
I did not hear sounds of ~~no~~ any
fighting — After advancing some 500
yards we found ourselves up against
German barbed wire — about 10ˣ wide
but very knocked about — ~~Although~~
There was a heavy mist on.
~~About the time this~~ We got through the
wire quite close (10ˣ) to German trenches.
to At this time Irish & to our right & N.
Lancs. to our left (both slightly to the rear)

6

were heavily bombed by the Germans —
with gas and smoke bombs —
Our Infantry started firing at Germans
at very close range.
After a short time they retired.
My ½ section retired with infantry
about 80ˣ into a shell hole. Lt Fisher
disappeared at this period — (before retirement)
We were then surrounded by bodies of
North Lancs. Liverpool Irish and 1/4 Kings'
Own. from the right —
They all appeared to have lost all direction,
& had no officers —
After some few minutes, everyone retired
to own advanced trench —
About 12 noon I had information from adj.
Irish / that Kings Own were held up on
right and wanted support. I took my
two guns up to the right (S of GUILLEMONT
TRONES) Road where I took up positions
in conjunction with Rt. ½ section —
As there were many Lewis guns here, I
retired to original position whence both
guns got targets on bodies of Germans
coming across from GUINCHY to QUARRY.
Fire seemed to be very effective —
I reported to Capt Saintsenus at about 7. p. m.
who ordered me to remain in positions taken
up. We were relieved at 1. A.M. 9/8/16.

Lce. Cpl. Parkinson G. in charge of left gun
states " ~~on retiring from~~ I heard order given
to retire from my right. On retiring
the Irish ↑2ⁿᵈ line bore to their right, towards
Railway — I did not see them again — nor
did I see any reinforcements go up.

Sgt Collinson says "as soon as mist cleared
German snipers started from their
front line — from Guillemont Trones road,
and from quarry —

Pte. Newton in charge of Rt. gun. Concurs.

Sgt Pye in charge of Rt half section
of No. 3 Section states —
  We advanced with 2ⁿᵈ line of L. Irish.
and North Lancs (who appeared to
be mixed up together) to be got
through the German wire up to the
parapet without any resistance — Bombs
(smoke & a few gas) were thrown by enemy
on my left. Great confusion ensued, &
finally, Infantry retired — towards ARROW
HEAD COPSE — I retired my half section
by bounds taking up positions in shell
holes till I arrived in advanced trench.
I then sent No 1. gun back to TRONES

8

WOOD trench as it had only 1 man
(Pte. Fairbrother) left on it —
Took up position in advanced trench, which
was then held by North Lancs Rgt —
(I did not see any Irish) When mist
lifted, I saw 2 parties of Germans
coming at double from direction of
GUINCHY (I am not sure whether from
village or from a trench between the villages)
Fire was opened, & satisfactory result
obtained — Another party attempted to dig
themselves in, in same direction, they were
made to desist. (Range 800ˣ)

Pte. Fairbrother. only man left of No.
8 gun. concurs —

Pte. Clark in charge of No 8 gun.
says he thinks that there were a few
Irish on left of party holding advanced
trench. There did not seem to be any
fighting S. of GUILLEMONT TRONES Road.

4.

No. 1 Section was allotted to H.Q. Coy as
Commander Lt Pursell.
Orders to form strong point S.E. & S.E. of Village
Left half section was under 2/Lt. he Diarmid
Left gun was under Sgt. Whitwell. The Coy
(my gun) went over with 2nd line (No 11 Platoon "C")
about 100x S. GUILLEMONT TRÔNES Road.
We advanced till at 20x behind No 9 Platoon
(which was leading the attack) and which
had been stopped by the enemy wire. This
platoon was had not been fired on
until it had reached the wire. A
very heavy M.G. & bomb fire (smoke & gas)
was opened on them on their arrival at
the wire. (a wounded man told me that
this wire was very thick and breast high).
They retired a second line of attack &
there reformed. A bomb attack was
then made, in the course of which a report
was received that the enemy were advancing
down the GUILLEMONT TRÔNES Road, on
our left. "B" Coy & a few of "C" were left
to meet this attack which proved to be
friendly troops. Orders were then given
for retirement into our own front line trench
and no section were remained there till
 Orders were given

to leave advance trench to avoid our own 10.
Artillery bombardment.
Position was taken up W of ARROW HEAD
COPSE — Polewood 4.a.m. 9.8.16.
M.G. fire came, I think, from the front.
Pte. Storey was also with this gun —
The attack was hung up by enemy
barbed wire — which was well made
& not much damaged — I did not
notice its depth.
M.G. fire seemed to come from Right
flank from strong point, heavily
enfilading our line —

Sgt. Bennett was with right gun
of the half section.
I started with leading platoon — We
arrived at the enemy wire, without being
fired on — On arrival a heavy M.G.
bomb and rifle fire was opened on us.
We retired with Infantry on 2nd line
about 15 to 20ˣ in rear — A second
attack was made (by bombs) but Infantry
were again driven back — I did not go
up with this 2nd attack — I then
discovered my gun was damaged.
I then saw Lieut. McDiarmid rallying
the Infantry for another attack, which
he led — but which was again unsuccessful

At this point information was
received that of attack on our left
flank — we faced round (with B
Coy.) but it proved to be friendly
troops — Word was then passed up to
return on to own advanced trench —
Remainder of narration same as left
gun —

I think enemy M.G. fire came from
our right front, from ridge N. by E.
of ARROW HEAD COPSE —

Pte. Dodge was with left gun of
right ½ section — He states.
I was with my gun — we went over with
front line of attack — which reached
German barbed wire (about 4.15?)
about 200ˣ in front of own line —
On reaching German wire a heavy
M.G. bomb (smoke & a large amount
of gas) & rifle fire was opened.
Platoon retired but bombers remained
& fought for about ¼ hour — they
then retired & I retired with them,
when I heard gun & tripod
were left behind (No 1 & 2 both wounded)
& Pte. Henderson & I returned for gun,
but were then unable to return to
own trench, so we lay in a shell hole

hole with Cpl. Montgomery, until our
artillery opened onto us & killed 3 men
near us — We then made a bolt for it —
~~around~~ I do not know how deep the
wire was. M.G. fire seemed to come from
our left. also the sniping — (This would
be E end of ridge N by E of ARROW HEAD
COPSE, A) We returned to our trench
about 4 p.m —

Lt. Purnell in charge of Right Gun
says — ~~to ~~
he advanced with the first wave of Inf.
to about 15ˣ of German wire, where
owing to heavy fire — (M.G. Rifle and
smoke & gas bomb) we had to retire with
Infantry, till reinforced by 2ⁿᵈ wave.
We endeavoured to mount our gun, but
had 3 gun numbers knocked out. We
got to ground in a shell hole.
Bombers were meanwhile bombing the
German parapet — but were mostly
knocked out. Pte Kirkham, of my gun,
then joined bombers, but all retired
on own advance trench.
Pte Kirkham cannot say what depth of wire
there was —
M.G. fire came from our left. 20ˣ
(~~A~~ N by E of ARROW H. Copse - ? A.)

No. 4 Section   Right:

Orders to take up a position near
S.30 B73 whence to bring fire
to bear across E face of GUILLEMONT

Capt. Santorin was in charge of left
half section —
Position taken up in support trench.
At 3.50 A.M. guns commenced to
advance past advanced trench —
King's Own got too much to
th left after leaving trench. leaving
large gap between their right flank
and sunk road
At 4.15 A.M. when advanced line
was some 50ˣ to 60ˣ in front of trench
& barrage was still on. M.G. fire and
heavy bomb fire was opened by enemy
(gas & smoke bombs)
Guns took up positions in shell
holes in front of own wire —
Infantry made 2 or 3 attempts to
attack but were each time repulsed,
& finally fell back into own trench.
They attempted to dig an advanced line
70 yards in front of line but
were unable to do so.
On their retiring M.G. also retired.

14

into advanced trench, & took up positions therein. Capt. Sartorius then took over command of Batalion —

I am of the opinion that German M. Guns. were situated near sunk Road — That enemy wire was not reached, (but only own concertina wire) by right flank of King's Own — & that Artillery barrage was well behind enemy position, & that consequently enemy opened fire on advancing infantry before they attacked, while they were still crawling out to take up attacking position —

Sgt. Brooks in charge of left gun says that he is of the opinion that right flank of attack only just passed own wire, if that, & agrees that M.G. fire was from SUNK ROAD. — I took over command of left ½ section from Capt. Sartorius. At about 10 A.M. one gun retired into support trench to avoid artillery bombardment (own) The other remained in position — Relieved at 4 A.M. 9/8/16.

Pte. Chatterton. in charge of No. 2 gun states. that he ~~arrived~~ reached

15

German wire — about 30ˣ in front of own
wire — enemy wire was undamaged
by our artillery & ~~from~~ thick —
he thinks German M.G. was on
right of sunken road —
At about 11.30 A.M. he got a target on
Germans on parapet, left of the sunken
road and about ~~~~ from ARROW
HEAD COPSE — N by E

2 Lt. Hartington was in charge of Rt.
half section to which 1 spare gun was
~~attached~~ — he says.
My section advanced level with Left
half section, and came under fire
at same time — we passed off to the
right and took up positions in the road,
in front of own barricade, about 30ˣ
from enemy barricade — The enemy
bombed us and being unprotected
we retired to own ~~~~ barricade with
a bombing post of 5ᵗʰ Kings Own
he took up positions to cover own digging
party to our left flank.
we were forced to retire owing to own
artillery bombarding own barricade —
he took up positions in advanced trench
to cover own line — Relieved 4.10 a.m.
9/8/16

I did not notice any german wire —
Enemy M.G. seemed to be ⟨struck⟩ to the
right of the road not more than 60ˣ from
road — Enemy snipers very good, chiefly
from & from near barricade —
There appeared to be a ⟨struck⟩ trench parallel
to the road on our left of road — ⟨struck⟩
S of barricade —
There was c.w.e. with right and left Btns.
⟨struck⟩ I am of the opinion that
attacking troops got too far to their left.

Pte. W. Johnston in charge of left gun says
I only saw our own wire — no enemy wire —
Pte. S. Hargreaves — concurs.

Pte. E Pearson ⟨struck⟩ to add —
thinks sniping came from the left of the
road —

War Diary

of

164 Machine Gun Company

1st September to 30th September 1916

Army Form C. 2118.

WAR DIARY
or
INTELLIGENCE SUMMARY.
(Erase heading not required.)

1st Lt Infantry Robert Mackwin Gurty

Place	Date	Hour	Summary of Events and Information	Remarks and references to Appendices
Camp No. Albert-Amiens Road	1/9/16		Training for Trench Warfare	
	2/9/16		2nd Lt J.J. Grendelle reported for duty	
	3/9/16			
	4/9/16			
	5/9/16		Moved to bivouacs at F.13.A. Company paraded p.m. 5 P.M.	
	6/9/16		No 3rd & 4th sections moved off to trenches in vicinity of Stormy. No 1 Section kept up supports in Quarry Trench on reserve No 2 Section remained at the Quarry	
QUARRY at BARNAFAY WOOD	7/9/16		No. 1 Sect. carried out an indirect overhead fire from FOLLY TRENCH. Enemy artillery retaliates on trench held by No. 3 Sect. Casualties 1 killed 4 wounded.	
"	8/9/16		No. 2 Sect. relieved No. 3 Sect. 11 a.m. At 5:50 p.m. No 1 & 2 Sects attacked STOUT TRENCH Casualties 2 killed 8 wounded (includ 2 Officer) — 1 gun put out of action. + VAT ALLEY.	
"	9/9/16		1 Sect in PILSEN LANE — 1 Sect in FOLLY TRENCH. Casualties 4 wounded Sect lying in Comm. trench (LONGUEVAL AV.) NY BN HQ had 1 gun blown up & 1 put out of action Casualties 1 killed 4 wounded	
"	10/9/16		No. 3 Sect. (2 guns & 10 men) set out with 26o's of Kings Own to execute a bombing raid on HOP ALLEY 5:15 a.m. Raid failed owing to trenches being so battered as to be unrecognisable. Casualties 1 N.C.O. wounded 1 man missing. This Section brought in an extra gun. Other Section in PILSEN LANE & STOUT TRENCH	

WAR DIARY or INTELLIGENCE SUMMARY

Army Form C. 2118.

Place	Date Sept 1916	Hour	Summary of Events and Information	Remarks and references to Appendices
Delville Wd.	11th	6 p.m.	6 p.m. No. 3 Sect. sent up to cover working party making strong pt. in DELVILLE WOOD. Two guns then took up position in strong pt. Other sections in 22 Avenue, PILSEN LANE & STOUT TRENCH.	
"	12th & 13th	12 midnt to 6 a.m.	Coy. Relieved & moved to camp at Becordel	
Becordel Ribemont	13th	9.30 am – 2.50 pm	Moved from camp to billets in Ribemont. Arrived at Ribemont. 2/Lt RENZECRY & 2/Lt ANSELL arrived from base. Lieut. BELLERBY arrived from Hd. Qrs. Guns overhauled & kit inspection. Remunging and 3 complete sections.	
"	14th		Inspection of billets & maniquer lines by Brig. Gen'l. Stockwell. Stunts submitted for approval.	
"	15th		Inspection of billets & maniquer lines by Brig. Gen'l Stockwell.	
"	16th	12.30 p.m.	1½ hours notice to move. 3.30 p.m. Arrived at BUIRE & settled into billets. Lt. STOCKWELL	
Buire	"	3.30 pm	Arrived from base. Major SARTORIUS, Lieut. BELLERBY, 2/Lt HARRIS. JAMES all from Depot of RIBEMONT Wd.	
Becordel	17th	10 p.m. – 11.30 pm	Church Parade. Moved to camp over BECORDEL. 25 O.R. reinforcements arrived.	
Quarry Mametz	18th 19th	4.0 am 5.0 pm	Moved to QUARRY near MONTAUBAN Moved to camp near MAMETZ. Poor accommodation.	
York Tr. nr. Longueval	20th	6 a.m.	Moved to YORK TRENCH. Shelling by H.E. & gas shells considerable, increasing towards night.	
"	21st	2 a.m.	Ration limber blown up. Gas shells ended mid-day. 2/Lt BALL joined from base. Section training. Reorganised into 4 sections again.	
"	22nd		Section training. Overhauling ammunition. Quiet day.	
"	23rd		Section training. Overhauling ammunition. Quiet day.	
"	24th		Major SARTORIUS sick. Lieut SARTORIUS took command of 165? Bde. in SWITCH TRENCH for Company. Then two sections to be placed at disposal of	
Switch Tr. N. & Flers	25th	4.0 a.m.	Company moved in accordance with order & was taken reserve for the attack on GIRD & GUEUDECOURT. Major SARTORIUS evacuated from YORK TR. sick to hospital. Lieut BELLERBY took command.	
"	26th		Remainder of Company moved up to SWITCH TR. Relief of 165 M.G. Coy. in SMOKE TR & GIRD TR. 2/Lt STOKWELL to hospital shell shock. Sgt OWEN took command of No. 1 Sn.	
"	27th	—	Relief of 165 M.G. Coy in SUNKEN Rd at dawn preparatory to attack by 16th Rifle.	

Army Form C. 2118.

WAR DIARY
or
INTELLIGENCE SUMMARY.
(Erase heading not required.)

Instructions regarding War Diaries and Intelligence Summaries are contained in F. S. Regs., Part II. and the Staff Manual respectively. Title pages will be prepared in manuscript.

Place	Date	Hour	Summary of Events and Information	Remarks and references to Appendices
FLERS	27.9.16		Coln. 2Lt WALLIS-JAMES took to Hospital. Sections in front line for attack :- No 1 Section under Lt. OWEN. 2 guns No. 4 Sn. under 2Lt ANSELL. 2 guns No. 3 Sn. under Sgt PYE. The whole controlled by 2Lt HARTINGTON. Commencing barrage for by No. 2 Sn. (in reserve) under 2Lt GARF. Casualties in going over the top, No. 1 Sn. 1 wounded remainder nil. Cool + daring work by Sgt OWEN. Excellent work by 2Lt HARTINGTON, informing + reporting. Defence scheme. Communication excellent. Casualties: 1 sgt. + killed. 1 wounded.	
		6.0 p.m.	Relief of front line sections by reserve sections. 10 reinforcements arrived – carried up rations.	
	28.9.16		Heavy bombardment of front line. 1 team, No. 2 Sn. missing believed blown up but found in the evening. Casualties comparatively small. Company relieved by 125th M.G. Coy. at 6.0 p.m. Casualties on relief severe. Reported No. 3 Sn. on Switch road. Company moved to camp near MAMETZ.	
MAMETZ DERMAN COURT	29.9.16	2.0 pm	Company moved to billets in DERMANCOURT. Arrived 4.30 p.m.	
"	30.9.16		Overhauling equipment + gun kit.	

CONFIDENTIAL

Vol 9

War Diary
of
164th M. G. Coy.
for the period
1st to 31st October 1916

Army Form C. 2118.

WAR DIARY
or
INTELLIGENCE SUMMARY

(Erase heading not required.)

164 M.G.C.

Place	Date	Hour	Summary of Events and Information	Remarks and references to Appendices
DERNANCOURT.	Oct 1.	10 A.M.	Rifle Inspection – Inspection of billets, preparatory to moving to new area.	
		2 P.M.	Entrained at Edge Hill Station.	
L'ETOILE.		8 P.M.	Arrived LONGPRÉ – marched to L'ETOILE.	
	2.	6 A.M.	Reveille – parade at 7 A.M. moved off 7.30 A.M. – entrained LONGPRÉ at 8.30 A.M.	
POPERINGHE.		9 P.M.	arrived at HAZEBROUCK marched to POPERINGHE.	
	3.	10 A.M.	Paraded for C.O. inspection.	
		3 P.M.	Paraded for pay.	
	4.	7 A.M.	Reveille – No. 1 Section moved off 8.30 A.M. to H.6.b.4.2. – remaining sections cleaned billets, stacked timber. – Left POPERINGHE at 12.15 P.M. –	
BRANDHOEK.		1 P.M.	Took over Camp H.7.a.1.3. from 86 M.G. Coy. – 3 teams of No.1 Section returned to Coy. H.Q. at 6.30 P.M.	
	5.	7 A.M.	Reveille	
		9 A.M.	Rifle & gun inspection by sections – belt filling	
		2 P.M.	Section parades.	
	6.	7 A.M.	Reveille	
		9 A.M.	Reorganization of Sections – Gun drill	
		2 P.M.	Action of Mechanism – care & cleaning of guns.	
	7.	6.30 A.M.	Reveille – Physical training	
		9 A.M.	Inspection of Smoke Helmets, Smoke Helmet Drill –	
		2 P.M.	Mechanism & Stoppages	

Army Form C. 2118.

WAR DIARY
or
INTELLIGENCE SUMMARY
(Erase heading not required.)

Instructions regarding War Diaries and Intelligence Summaries are contained in F.S. Regs., Part II. and the Staff Manual respectively. Title Pages will be prepared in manuscript.

Place	Date	Hour	Summary of Events and Information	Remarks and references to Appendices
BRANDHOEK	Oct. 8	7.30 AM	Reveille	
		9.0 AM	Range practice	
		1.45 P.M.	Company parade for bathing.	
	9.	6.30 AM	Reveille. – Physical training.	
		9.0 AM	Range practice – firing with sight mounting two mounting practice in swinging traverse	
		2 P.M.	Issue of Box Respirators to all with same.	
	10.	6.30 AM	Reveille. – Packing of limbers	
		9.0 AM	Box Respirator Rifle & Trench Drill. –	
		2 P.M.	Advanced Drill.	
	11.	6.30 AM	Reveille. – Physical Training.	
		9.0 AM	Coy. paraded at Gas Chamber for Box Respirator Drill. – Trench drill	
			Advanced Drill. – Lecture on Map Reading by C.O. to N.C.O.s. –	
		2 AM	Inspection of Box Respirators. – Positing names wearing of	
			Pte Rogerson G. awarded Military Medal.	
	12.	6.30 AM	Reveille. – Physical training.	
		9.0 AM	Action from the limber – practising ammunition supply from limbers. –	
		5.0 P.M.	Section training – Stripping of Gun.	
	13.	6.30 AM	Reveille – Physical Training.	
		9.0 AM	Box Respirator & Gas Helmet Drill. –	
		10.30 AM	Presentation of Military Medal to Pte Fairbrother. –	

Army Form C. 2118.

WAR DIARY
or
INTELLIGENCE SUMMARY

(Erase heading not required.)

16 H.M.L. Coy

Instructions regarding War Diaries and Intelligence Summaries are contained in F. S. Regs., Part II. and the Staff Manual respectively. Title Pages will be prepared in manuscript.

Place	Date	Hour	Summary of Events and Information	Remarks and references to Appendices
BRANSHOEK	Oct 13	2 P.M.	Gun Drill – Trench drill in Respirators.	
	14	7.30 AM	Reveille	
		9 AM	Inspection of Service Helmets & Box Respirators. – Trench drill in Box Respirators	
			Cleaning of guns and spare parts & ammunition	
		2 P.M.	Packing of limbers.	
		6 P.M.	Moved off to relieve 16 S M.G.C. at YPRES – (right sector)	
		9.30		
YPRES	15		Situation normal – Casualties Nil. – Own guns on RAMPARTS, arrived 2 P.M. – relief completed	
	16		Situation normal – Indirect fire on RUPPRECHT F.M. and CROSS RDS control CHATEAU WOOD.	improvements to drainage of dug-outs & trenches were in support & those in front line
	17		Capt. M? Richardson took over command of Coy/Coy – situation normal – indirect fire on RUPPRECHT F.M. and CROSS ROADS (corner of FARM).	
	18		Situation normal – Indirect fire with RUPPRECHT F.M. CROSS RDS I. B26.d.9. FORKED RDS. I7a.D.3. Communication trench J.7b.26.d5.	
	19		Situation normal – improvement of emplacements and mountings – Indirect fire on RAILWAY (J.7.a). CHATEAU WOOD (J.13.a.5.9.) RUPPRECHT F.M. (CROSS RDS L. or FARM.	
	20		Situation normal – Indirect fire on WESTHOEK, point where German trench Crosses MENIN RD., RUPPRECHT F.M., Communication Tr. (J.7h.2.3.35.)	

2449   Wt. W4957/M90 750,000 1/16 J.B.C. & A. Forms/C.2118/12.

WAR DIARY or INTELLIGENCE SUMMARY

Army Form C. 2118.

Instructions regarding War Diaries and Intelligence Summaries are contained in F.S. Regs., Part II. and the Staff Manual respectively. Title Pages will be prepared in manuscript.

(Erase heading not required.)

Place	Date	Hour	Summary of Events and Information	Remarks and references to Appendices
YPRES.	Sept 21		Capt R Shardlow DSO to attend VIII Corps School - 2nd Lt Hopkins Fry and Corpl Burch Gratin joined. Situation normal - Indirect fire on WESTHOEK RIDGE N of Ry. ROULERS (J.13.d.3)	
	22		RAILWAY & TRENCHES (J.1.A.) COMMUNICATION TR. (J.7.C.28.35) and gas projector lately mounted in VERLORENHOEK Rd, WESTHOEK J.13.c.5.6 + various on Rly.	
	23	3.30pm	Relieved by 163 M.G.B.	
YPRES	24		Relieved 163 M.G.C. on left sector. 2nd & 3rd Bty not completed until 6 p.m. Garrison of guns - 2 guns in support, 2 in line. Improvements to drainage of trenches made by Situation normal - Indirect fire on C.29.b.5.9 to C.29.a.9.3, C.23.a.4.4, and BILL COTTAGE (I.66.25.80.) Situation normal - Indirect fire, searching road between C.29.b.6.3.30 to C.29.1.5, and searching of ZONNEBEEK Rd. (Con Road) to C.23.a.6.3.80.)	
	25			
	27.		Situation normal - searching light railway & road C.23.C.9.03.0 to C.23.d.9.05.5 - C.23.d.4.85. - Gun N7 caused fire because of drawing fire from retaliatory fire on WIELTJE - ST JEAN road. Prevented road C.20.b.5.30. to C.23.d.4.S.	
	28		Situation normal - Indirect fire on BOSSAERT FARM and traverses ROAD C.29.b.5.30 to C.23.d.1.S. - Completed repairs to 2d Emplacement. New alternative position No7 A 5 - Reflooring of emplacement No7 A	

Army Form C. 2118.

164 M.G. Coy

WAR DIARY
or
INTELLIGENCE SUMMARY

(Erase heading not required.)

Instructions regarding War Diaries and Intelligence Summaries are contained in F.S. Regs., Part II. and the Staff Manual respectively. Title Pages will be prepared in manuscript.

Place	Date	Hour	Summary of Events and Information	Remarks and references to Appendices
KAAIE	Oct 28 (cont'd)		Two others emplacement at PROMISE FARM - new one to dug out at A1 Situation normal - Indirect fire bearing ZONNEBEKE road & sweeping roads	
	29		BRIDGE H.V. to APPLE VILLA coord. C29 d.6.5.3b. to C23 d.1.5.	
	30		Situation normal - relieved by 166 M.G.C.	
BRANDHOEK	31	10 PM	Entrained at YPRES - arrived BRANDHOEK at 12 midnight. Encamped at H.T.9.A.3. General cleaning up of guns, spare parts, rifles, equipment, clothing &c.	

J.J. [signature]
2nd Lt
for o/c 164th Machine Gun Coy

CONFIDENTIAL

Vol 10

War Diary

of

164th Machine Gun Coy.

for period

1st November to 30th November 1916

Army Form C. 2118.

WAR DIARY
or
INTELLIGENCE SUMMARY of 1/6 4 Machine Gun Coy.

(Erase heading not required.)

Instructions regarding War Diaries and Intelligence Summaries are contained in F. S. Regs., Part II. and the Staff Manual respectively. Title Pages will be prepared in manuscript.

Place	Date	Hour	Summary of Events and Information	Remarks and references to Appendices
BRANDHOEK Hut 1.3	Nov 1	7.0	Physical training	
		9.0	Close order drill and cleaning	
		12.30		
		3pm	Brigade inspection	
		4pm		
	2	7.0am	Physical training	
		9.0	No 1 & 2 Section - Action trots on range and competitive firing	
		12.30pm	Revolver practice. Nos 3 & 4 section administration duties.	
		2.0pm	Tact. scheme for officers and Sgts. R. Gun drill for men order by O/Officer	
		3.0 pm		
	3.	7.0am	Physical training	
		9.0am	Carrying out of tactical scheme of 2/11/16	
		12.30pm	Gun drill and action against tanks under orderly Officer	
		2 pm	Lectures for officers	
		3.pm		
	4.	7.am	Physical training	
		9.am	Bathing. Musketry tests on range. Range firing revolver from tanks action from tanks	
		12.30pm	Tactical scheme for Offr & Sgts. Gun drill for Coy	
		2.pm		
		3pm		

Army Form C. 2118.

WAR DIARY
or
INTELLIGENCE SUMMARY of 1/4 Kings Own R...

(Erase heading not required.)

Instructions regarding War Diaries and Intelligence Summaries are contained in F. S. Regs., Part II. and the Staff Manual respectively. Title Pages will be prepared in manuscript.

Place	Date	Hour	Summary of Events and Information	Remarks and references to Appendices
BRANDHOEK	Nov 5	9.0 AM	Lecture for officers and N.C.Os.	
		11 AM	Company parade. Probably attended to by Lt Col Owen & Major General H.Q. followed by Kitchen Football Match	
		2.0 PM	Tactical scheme in cooperation with 2/5 Loyal N.L.R. and 1/4 Loyal North Lancs.	
	6.	9 AM to 12.30 PM		
		2 PM	Sectional tactical scheme for NCOs.	
		3 PM	Cleaning and overhauling guns & ammunition, Rest, filling and feeding of tubes.	
		5.30 PM	3 pieces of M.G. relief of 165 M.G.C. in the support sector	
		7.30 PM	Coy H.Q. established at I.9.c.14.0.	
YPRES	7		Situation normal - heavy hurricane concert barrage in fact n... postponed owing to the fog	
Right Sector	8		Situation normal 30,000 rounds...	
	9			
	10		Situation normal, firing of machine gun in I.11.5 and I.11.5 ... J.2.b.d 3.9.50	

Army Form C. 2118.

WAR DIARY
or
INTELLIGENCE SUMMARY of 104 Machine Gun Coy.

(Erase heading not required.)

Instructions regarding War Diaries and Intelligence Summaries are contained in F.S. Regs., Part II. and the Staff Manual respectively. Title Pages will be prepared in manuscript.

Place	Date	Hour	Summary of Events and Information	Remarks and references to Appendices
YPRES	Nov 11	2.15 P.M.	Heavy T.M. shelling of RAILWAY WOOD trenches at Ry. Wd. Mounted on Casualty - Pte. Tuddim killed. Rds fired 4000	
	12		Situation normal. Rds fired 3000	
	13	2 AM	M.G. emplacement at I.11.b broken by enemy fire. Heavy bombardment of R.W. WOOD Posts. Rds fired 4750.	
	14		Situation normal. Heavy firing by our M.Gs 5250 rds of Germans working parties at GREY RUIN and RUPPRECHT Fm & heights RY at I.6.a 60.55 along which enemy appeared to rend material.	
	15		Situation normal - Ammunition of tire on M.G. also enemy G.S. Waggon near trenches. Rds fired 5000	
	16		Situation normal - working party at RUPPRECHT Fm fired at with excellent results (Rds fired 4750)	
	17	11 pm	Situation normal - normal targets engaged - firing by day upon RUPPRECHT Fm 3550 Rds. Carrying out by Division of heavy bombardment enemy trenches M.Cs. Co-operated with attention to 2nd Army fired LAKE Fm ZIEL HOUSE &c for 7.15-65.59	
NAIE	18		Horses across to left Sector Relieved by 165 M.G. Coy, Relieved 166 M.G. Coy. Corpl. Richardson wounded, Pte Richardson wounded & removed.	

WAR DIARY or INTELLIGENCE SUMMARY

Army Form C. 2118.

Place	Date	Hour	Summary of Events and Information	Remarks and references to Appendices
KAAIE	Nov 19		Situation normal. CAMERON AV. & DRIVE shelled approx 12.30 no	
	20		Situation normal – During the day heavy fire on WHITE ROAD, no fire returned after 3 p.m	
	21		Situation normal – Firing from GREY RUIN & RUPPRECHT FARM 10/-	
	22		Searches R₉ and ZONNEBEKE R⁴ 500 rounds fired	
	23		L' Bell. by day left to attend Vin Corps School	
			Situation normal 4000 rounds fired on RUPPRECHT F. during night	
	24		Target S engaged RUIN FARM formerly know Capt McKenna proceeded on leave	
	25		9/Br Herting from Salk relieved ○ C Officers the formerly in command of the Coy. Coy fired 3500	
BRANDHOEK	26		Partial relief of Coy. Lecture 1 + 111 return to BRANDHOEK. Section 7 occupied RAILWAYS DUG-OUTS.	
		10.45pm	The advance of REIGERS BORG. Relief completed.	
	27		Cleaning of guns & equipment. Pay ng of Coy Erection of Galley and Cookhouse	
	28		Ringtone practice.	
	29		Inspection by Brigadier	
	30			

Vol XI

War Diary
of the
104th Machine Gun Company
for the period.
1st December to 31st December, 1916.

To Headquarters
   164 Inf. Bde.

164 COMPANY M.G. CORPS.
No: B62
DATE: 11.17

Herewith attached please find "War Diary" of this company for the month of December. 1916.

J.E. Hastington.
Lieut.

CAPTAIN
COMMDG: 164 COY: M.G. CORPS.

Army Form C. 2118.

WAR DIARY
or
INTELLIGENCE SUMMARY

(Erase heading not required.)

164 Machine Gun Coy

Instructions regarding War Diaries and Intelligence Summaries are contained in F.S. Regs., Part II. and the Staff Manual respectively. Title Pages will be prepared in manuscript.

Place	Date	Hour	Summary of Events and Information	Remarks and references to Appendices
BRANDHOEK	1916 Dec 1.	7-9.30 am	Physical Training	
		9-10 am	Revolver Instruction - Aiming & Loading	
		10-11 am	Squad Drill and Saluting Drill	
		11-12.30	Range Practice	
		2-3 pm	Section Parade, Change Gun Kit.	
			Relief of No 2 Section by No 3 Section on Ramparts.	
	Dec 2.	7-9.30	Physical Training	
		9-10.30	Close Order Drill - Guard Duties - Section Range Finders instructional Parade	
		10.45 12-30	Range Practice - Rifles.	
		2-3.30	Gun Kit Inspection & Belt Filling.	
	Dec 3.	9.30 am	Kit & Hut Inspection by C.O.	
		10.30 am	Church Parade.	
	Dec 4.	7.30 7.50	Physical Training	
		9-10	Close Order Drill	
		10-12.30	Revolver Practice	
		2.30	Coy Football match	
		7.30 7.50	Physical Training	
	Dec 5.	10.15-11.30		
		2 pm - 5 pm	"Stand To". Brigade tactical Exercise. Action to & to from Limbers	

Army Form C. 2118.

WAR DIARY
or
INTELLIGENCE SUMMARY
(Erase heading not required.)

164 Machine Gun Coy/

Place	Date	Hour	Summary of Events and Information	Remarks and references to Appendices
BRANDHOEK	Dec 6	7–7.45	Packing limbers	
		10 A.M.	Inspection by Corps Commander.	
		2–3 p.m.	Respirator Drill.	
	Dec.7	7.30 / 7.50	Physical Exercise	
		9–12.30	Preparation & cleaning of all Lewis Kit preparatory to moving into Trenches.	
		4 p.m.	Company moved up to Trenches.	
		8 p.m.	Relief of 165 Coy Completed. Section No. 1 — the Lehoofs (Ruins) " 2 — HELL FIRE CORNER (Right Sector) " 3 — RAILWAY WOOD (Centre Sector) " 4 — POTIJZE (Left Sector)	
YPRES	Dec 8		Situation Normal — nothing to report — no firing on account of Shoot until night of 10 inst to lull enemy into sense of false security	
"	– 9		Situation Normal — nothing to report. Capt. RICHARDSON returned from Class Watering our command of Coy.	

Army Form C. 2118.

WAR DIARY
or
INTELLIGENCE SUMMARY

(Erase heading not required.)

164 Machine Gun Coy

Place	Date	Hour	Summary of Events and Information	Remarks and references to Appendices
YPRES	Dec 10	—	Situation Normal.	
	" 11	4.57pm	In conjunction with Artillery, heavy Machine Gun fire on Tracks & Communications of enemy. 4 guns therefore opened out fire barrage at 4.57pm - 6.5p - 7.25pm and 9-35pm 2nd Shot very successful, every part our heavy aeroplane fire in support area. No of rounds fired 11,450	
	Dec 12	7.30 am	Relief of No 3 Section by No 1 Section on Railway Wood Sector. Situation Normal. — Number of Rounds fired 1650.	
	Dec 13	—	Situation Normal. — Number of Rounds fired 4750	
	Dec 14	—	Situation Normal — Minor shoot on Clapham Junction, Westhoek. Rounds fired 5500	
	Dec 15	3-45 4.45	Heavy hostile artillery fire directed on by HQ & Railway Wood. D.Y Barrage Round Railway Wood. Our artillery replied heavily. Rounds fired 4500.	
	Dec 16	—	Situation Normal — No of Rounds fired 4500.	
	Dec 17	—	Relieved by 165 M Gun Coy on Right Sector — Proceeded to Left Sector to relieve 166 M Gun Coy. No 1 Section to WIELTJE — No 2 Section ST JEAN — No 3 Section — CANAL BANK — No 4 Section — POTIZE. Rounds fired 2250	

Army Form C. 2118.

WAR DIARY
or
INTELLIGENCE SUMMARY

(Erase heading not required.)

164 Machine Gun Coy

Place	Date	Hour	Summary of Events and Information	Remarks and references to Appendices
KAAIE	Dec 18.	—	Situation Normal — 2250 Rounds fired	
	"19	—	Situation Normal — 4750 Rounds fired.	
	"20	—	Situation Normal — 4500 Rounds fired — Two Casualties - both killed by shell fired at Potyze.	
	"21	—	Situation Normal — Rounds fired 4,500.	
	22	—	Cooperation with Infantry & Artillery on raid made by 2 R.L. Regt. defensive targets on flanks & rear of enemy trenches engaged at stated times. Rounds fired 16,850. Retaliation finely heavy. No casualties. No 1 Section relieved at Westhof sector by No 3 Section. (Field Stockwell in) No 2 Section, less one gun, in reserve at Canal Bank. One gun at La Brique.	
	23.	—	Situation Normal — Rounds fired 4,500.	
	24	—	Situation Normal — Rounds fired 4,500.	
	25	—	Situation Normal — Rounds fired 4,500.	

Army Form C. 2118.

WAR DIARY
or
INTELLIGENCE SUMMARY. 164 M Gun Coy
(Erase heading not required.)

Instructions regarding War Diaries and Intelligence Summaries are contained in F. S. Regs., Part II. and the Staff Manual respectively. Title pages will be prepared in manuscript.

Place	Date	Hour	Summary of Events and Information	Remarks and references to Appendices
KAAIE	Dec 26	—	Situation normal – Capt Richardson proceeded to VIII Corps School – Lieut Clark proceeded to 55th Div School – Lieut Arlington took command.	
	27	—	2/Lieut Addows reported for Duty. Relief of Company by 166 Coy. — No 1 Section took up position on Ramparts. Remainder of Coy to BRANDHOEK	
BRANDHOEK	28 to 30		Company Training	
	31		Capt Richardson returned & took over command. Company Christmas Dinner & Concert.	

Signed: A. Richardson CAPTAIN
COMMDG: 164 COY: M.G. CORPS.

Diary
of the
[illegible]
[illegible]
[illegible]

Army Form C. 2118.

WAR DIARY
or
INTELLIGENCE SUMMARY 164 Machine Gun Coy.

(Erase heading not required.)

Place	Date	Hour	Summary of Events and Information	Remarks and references to Appendices
BRANDHOEK	Jan 1		No parades.	J.J.
"	2	9am	Route march — Relief of No 1 Section at RAMPARTS by No 4 Sect.	J.J.
	3		Company parade	J.J.
	4		Company went through Gas Chamber	J.J.
	5		Company Training	
	6			J.J.
	6		Cleaning of Gun Kit & preparatory to moving up into Trenches.	N.L.
		4pm	Coy move to Trenches. Lieut Jones returns from leave	
YPRES RT. BDE Sector		10pm	Relief completed — Disposition of Guns taken} Section 1 ECOLE} Section 2 HELLFIRE CORNER No 3 Section POTIJZE (High (10th) — No 4 Section RAILWAY WOOD	
	7		Rounds fired 6000 — Situation Normal	
	8		Rounds fired 5250 — Situation Normal	
	9		Increased artillery on both sides — Gapping carried out between YPRES Ramparts & Ecole. SAA fired 5250 — H-tent Onsell ypres on leave	J.J.
	10		Continuation of Artillery bombardment, M. Gun Cooperation with trench mortars in 4th Brigade Sector. Heavy bombardment between 12 noon & 3pm. A Battery in 4th Brigade trenches knock hanging out T.O.R. K.C.L.E. British trench B.25. Rounds fired 6125.	J.H.

WAR DIARY or INTELLIGENCE SUMMARY

Army Form C. 2118.

(Erase heading not required.)

Instructions regarding War Diaries and Intelligence Summaries are contained in F.S. Regs., Part II. and the Staff Manual respectively. Title Pages will be prepared in manuscript.

Place	Date	Hour	Summary of Events and Information	Remarks and references to Appendices
YPRES	11 Jan		Situation much quieter - Enemy taking less interest - Rounds fired [illegible]	
	12			12
	13			13
	14		Situation Normal — Rounds fired 5250	
	15		Enemy more active than usual - Rounds fired 5000	
	16		Situation Normal - Rounds fired 4750	
	17		He Coy relieved by the 116 H/Bn Coy - Messrs B. McA. & S [illegible] Snipers remain in positions at [illegible]	
	18		Coy training. Transport mate pack harness to less than 3 lengths	
	19			
	20		Coy training - Report small reports from Guns	E
	21		Brigade Bomb[illegible] inspection	
	22		Coy training - Transport Pers now consist of the WL on foot Clerk & [illegible] from Battalion	J. McA.
	23			K.H

Army Form C. 2118.

WAR DIARY
or
INTELLIGENCE SUMMARY

164 Machine Gun Coy.

(Erase heading not required.)

Place	Date	Hour	Summary of Events and Information	Remarks and references to Appendices
S Camp	24		Company training	
	27		Brigade Commander Inspection of Coy on march	
	28		Lieut Clark & 2 Lieut Aldous proceed on Anti-Aircraft course	
	29-31		Company training	
			36364/6 Pte Jones F and 33595 Pte Bennn awarded Military Medal	

J E Hartington
Lieut.

Confidential

War Diary.

of

164th Machine
Gun Coy.

Feb 1917

69.
70.
71.
72.
73.
74.
75.
76.
77.
78.
79.
80.
81.
82.
83.
84.
85.
86.
87.
88.
89.
90.
91.
92.
93.
94.
95.
96.
97.
98.
99.
100.
101.
102.
103.
104.

Army Form C. 2118.

WAR DIARY
or
INTELLIGENCE SUMMARY

(Erase heading not required.)

104 Machine Gun Coy

Instructions regarding War Diaries and Intelligence Summaries are contained in F. S. Regs., Part II. and the Staff Manual respectively. Title Pages will be prepared in manuscript.

Place	Date	Hour	Summary of Events and Information	Remarks and references to Appendices
"S" Camp	Feb 1st to Feb 3rd		Company Training	
	Feb 4		Company Entrained at Guessemarket Station for Bellezelle arrived 6.15 pm. Transport travelled by road leaving S. Camp 7.30 A.M.	
BELLEZELLE	Feb 5		Arrival of Transport 4 P.M.	
	" 8		Lieut Gale to Hospital (Rental incident)	
	" 10		Lieut Gale return to duty.	
	" 11		2/Lieut Smyth A.T. Cooper-Smith & Officer reinforcements report for duty from Base.	Company training
	12		2/Lieut Wallis James to Hospital Unwell to Anti Aircraft Course.	
	13		Brigade Night Operations	
	14		Inspection of Company in Tactical Exercises by G.O.C.	
	15		Transport left at 11 A.M. for ABANZHOEK	

Army Form C. 2118.

WAR DIARY
or
INTELLIGENCE SUMMARY
(Erase heading not required.)

164 Machine Gun Coy

Instructions regarding War Diaries and Intelligence Summaries are contained in F.S. Regs., Part II. and the Staff Manual respectively. Title Pages will be prepared in manuscript.

Place	Date	Hour	Summary of Events and Information	Remarks and references to Appendices
BOLLEZEELE	Feb 16	9pm	Company entrained at BOLLEZEELE for BRANDHOEK Camp arrived and relieved the 116th Coy at 2.30pm Transport take over lines at S Camp	JWH
BRANDHOEK	17		Transport moved from "S" camp to Feb nos Transport lines at BRANDHOEK from 116 Coy.	JWH
			Nos 1 & 3 Sections moved up to YPRES and took over positions in RAMPARTS from 116 Coy.	
	17-21		Coy less two Sections carry out Training at Camp	JWH
	21		2/Lieut Ansell returns from Anti-Aircraft Course	JWH
	22		Nos 2 & 4 Sections relieve Nos 1 & 3 in Ramparts	JWH
	22-23		2/Lt Wallis James returns from Hospital. Company Training	JWH
	23		Coy went through Div. Gas Chamber Two guns attacked 2/5 Lanc Fusilrs in Tactical Scheme	JWH

2449 Wt. W14957/M90 750,000 1/16 J.B.C. & A. Forms/C.2118/12.

Army Form C. 2118.

WAR DIARY
or
INTELLIGENCE SUMMARY

(Erase heading not required.)

Instructions regarding War Diaries and Intelligence Summaries are contained in F.S. Regs., Part II. and the Staff Manual respectively. Title Pages will be prepared in manuscript.

16/4 Machine Gun Coy

Place	Date	Hour	Summary of Events and Information	Remarks and references to Appendices
BRANDHOEK	24		Preparation for trenches	J.R.
	25		Coy relieved 166 Coy in Left Brigade Sector. Relief complete 10.45pm. Disposition No 1 Section less 2 guns ST JEAN	J.R.L.
			" 2 " + 1 gun from No1 section WIELTJE	
			" 3 " " POTIJZE	
			" 4 " CANAL BANK	
LEFT BRIGADE SECTOR	26		Situation Normal — Canal Bank shelled — one country (Adver. Dre.) became untenable — allocation 2 minute bursts Gun position C.27d (Adver. Dre) became untenable owing to enemy shrapnel fire when machine gun opened fire.	J.R.L.
	27		2/Lt J Aldous to Divisional School Course	J.R.
	28		Situation normal — one gun placed in new section — Three guns relieved & taken over by 166 Coy at Hell-Bear & POTIJZE	J.R.L.

D. R. Lawderman
O.C. 16/4 M.G.C.

2449 Wt. W14957/M90 750,000 1/16 J.B.C. & A. Forms/C.2118/12.

WO/14

WAR DIARY
164th Machine Gun Company
March 1917

Army Form C. 2118.

WAR DIARY
or
INTELLIGENCE SUMMARY.
(Erase heading not required.)

104 Machine Gun Coy

Instructions regarding War Diaries and Intelligence Summaries are contained in F. S. Regs., Part II. and the Staff Manual respectively. Title pages will be prepared in manuscript.

Place	Date	Hour	Summary of Events and Information	Remarks and references to Appendices
KAAIE	March 1		Shelling of Canal Bank - ST JEAN - YPRES heavily shelled - Rounds fired 4500 from M.G.	J.H
LEFT Bde Sector	2		Situation Normal - Rounds fired 4500	J.H
	3		Situation Normal - Shelling of St JEAN - 2/Lt Cooper-Smith to Hospital	J.H
	4		Situation Normal - Shelling of YPRES	J.H
	5		Gun team in reserve at Canal Bank occupy new emplacement at C.28.i	J.H
			- 16 Guns in line - 1 O.R. casualty (M.G bullet wound in L.H arm)	
	6		Situation Normal	J.H
	7		Situation Normal - 3 O.R. Reinforcements from Base	J.H
	8 } 12 }			J.H
	13		Situation Normal - 4 O.R. Reinforcements from Base	J.H
	14 } 15 }		Situation Normal	J.H
	16		Company relieved by 166 M.Gun Coy Sections 1 & 3 move to L line Defences	J.H
BRANDHOEK	17		Relief complete 6 A.M.	J.H

Army Form C. 2118.

WAR DIARY
or
INTELLIGENCE SUMMARY.
(Erase heading not required.)

164 Machine Gun Coy.

Place	Date	Hour	Summary of Events and Information	Remarks and references to Appendices
BRANDHOEK	17-21		Company training	K.4.
	18		2/Lt J Wallis-James to Barriers.	K.4
	22		Inspection of Company by Brigadier-General.	K.4
	22nd		2/Lt T. Cooper-Smith returns to duty from Hospital. Sections Nos 2 & 4 relieve Nos 1 & 3 sections in 1st line Defences.	K.4
	27		Relief of 166 M. Gun Coy in Left Brigade Sector.	K.4
LEFTSETON	28		Situation Normal - 2/Lieut Mellows returns to duty from Div. School.	K.4
	29		Situation Normal	K.4
	30		Lieut R.M. Gale to Div. School.	K.4

Aur. Richardson
Capt
Cmg 164th Machine Gun Coy

CONFIDENTIAL.

WAR DIARY

of

164TH MACHINE GUN COMPANY

APRIL 1917

Army Form C. 2118.

WAR DIARY
or
INTELLIGENCE SUMMARY.
(Erase heading not required.)

164 Machine Gun Company

Instructions regarding War Diaries and Intelligence Summaries are contained in F. S. Regs., Part II. and the Staff Manual respectively. Title pages will be prepared in manuscript.

Place	Date	Hour	Summary of Events and Information	Remarks and references to Appendices
LEFT BRIGADE SECTOR	April 1-5		Situation Normal – Inclement Wr. –	A/24
	5th		Inter-section Relief – 2/Lt Arwell relieves 2/Lt Smyth	K/4
	6th		Situation Normal – 2/Lt Smyth to Artillery 3 day course.	K/4
	7-9		Situation Normal – 2/Lt Wallis Jones returns to duty from course	K/4
			at CAMIERS – 2/Lt Smyth rejoins from Artillery Course.	K/3
	10-15		Situation Normal – Heavy shelling in vicinity of CANAL BANK	K/3
	16		Company relieved by 116 M. Gun Coy on Right Sub-sector and 166 M.G.	K/4
			on Right Sub-Sector & Coy Relief proceeded to L Camp.	K/4
L. Camp.	17.		Company proceeded to HOUTKERQUE by route march.	K/4
HOUTKERQUE	18-21		Company Training	K/4
	22		Route March to NOORDPEENE	K/4
NOORDPEENE	23		" " " HELLEBROUCQ	K/4
HELLEBROUCQ	24		Lt Gale rejoins Company from Lewis Gun School	K/4
	24-30		Company Training on Area – Range – Quarries.	K/4

A. Richardson Capt
Comg 164 M.G. Coy

CONFIDENTIAL.

164th MACHINE GUN COMPANY.

WAR DIARY.

MAY 1917.

Army Form C. 2118.

WAR DIARY
or
INTELLIGENCE SUMMARY.
(Erase heading not required.)

164 Machine Gun Coy.

Instructions regarding War Diaries and Intelligence Summaries are contained in F.S. Regs., Part II. and the Staff Manual respectively. Title pages will be prepared in manuscript.

Place	Date	Hour	Summary of Events and Information	Remarks and references to Appendices
HELLEBROUCQ	1-2/8/17		Company training.	
"	3-5		Brigade Training Scheme.	
NOORDPEENE	6.		Coy. proceeded by march route to NOORDPEENE staying there overnight.	
BRANDHOEK Left Pos^n Sector	7.		Coy. proceeded by route march to ARNEKE entrained for POPERINGHE marched to BRANDHOEK	
	8.		Coy. relieved 166 M.G. Coy in Left Bttn. position at YPRES. Disposition 106 M.G. Coy at front/reserve	
	9.		in WELTJE MINE Dug Out. 12 guns in support and 4 in reserve.	
			A small MG Coy. to take up duties as Brigade Conducting Officer Situation normal. Several casualties	
			Lt Knott joins Coy. from Base.	
	10-11.		Situation normal - wanted indirect fire - 2nd Lt Coppersmith left Coy to take up duties	
	12.		as Brigade Conducting Officer. Situation normal wanted indirect fire.	
	13.		Situation normal wanted indirect fire. 1 O.R. wounded Pte HUGHES G.O.W. Regt	
	14.		Situation normal wanted indirect fire. 1 O.R. (att^d from 1/4 E. Lancs Reg.) No. 35 G.A.W.	
	15.		2/Lt Brown joined Coy. from Base.	
			Situation normal wanted indirect fire.	
	16.		Situation normal wanted indirect fire. Capt H. Nichols (154 M.G. Coy) assumed	
	17.		command of the Coy. Situation normal. Wanted indirect fire	

Army Form C. 2118.

WAR DIARY
or
INTELLIGENCE SUMMARY.
(Erase heading not required.)

164 Machine Gun Coy.

Instructions regarding War Diaries and Intelligence Summaries are contained in F. S. Regs. Part II. and the Staff Manual respectively. Title pages will be prepared in manuscript.

Place	Date	Hour	Summary of Events and Information	Remarks and references to Appendices
Kopf Odd Sector	18/5/17	—	Situation normal - usual indirect fire. Capt. Richardson & S/Cpl Coy to proceed to Base for UK.	
	19		Hargreaves posted (G.A.W.)	
			Situation normal - usual indirect fire.	
	20.		Situation normal - Co-operation with Artillery + T.M. in concentrated fire bearing on Kl. Slack. Proceeded on leave. Cpl Coll T.H. OR proceeded to Course at Camiers	
	20-2.		Situation normal - usual indirect fire	
	23.		Situation normal - usual indirect fire. Re-distribution of sectors - new Bdy. Boundary. Three guns of 166 M.G. Coy attd: for discipline this & then + 10 of Coy guns in support positions - both guns of Coy at Hqrs in reserve	
	24 night		3 guns of 166 R.G. Coy calibrated by this of 164 Coy.	
	24.		Situation normal - usual indirect fire. Mr. Hollington proceeds on leave	
	25.		Situation normal - usual indirect fire	
	26.		3 guns of 166 M.G. Coy returned by 3 guns 164 M.G. Coy. On return attd: 118 M.G. Coy	
	27		Situation normal - usual indirect fire	
	28		Gun attd 101st M.G. Coy relieved - situation normal - usual indirect fire	
	29-30		Situation normal - usual indirect fire. 30th Coy barrage scheme	
	31.		Situation normal - usual indirect fire	

Richard Carlyon
Capt. O.C. 164 M.G. Coy

CONFIDENTIAL.

164th MACHINE GUN COMPANY.

WAR DIARY for the

month of JUNE.

Army Form C. 2118.

WAR DIARY
or
INTELLIGENCE SUMMARY.
(Erase heading not required.)

164 Machine Gun Co Infantry

Place	Date	Hour	Summary of Events and Information	Remarks and references to Appendices
Left Boesinghe	June 1		Situation normal – Lt James to Hospital – Lt Clark from leave.	J.104
	2		Situation normal	J.604
	3		Situation normal – Lieut Stockwell on leave.	J.303
		10.15pm	Heavy Tear & gas-shell bombardment of DEAD END.	J.10.4
	4-8		Situation normal – Lieut Cole reports for duty from Cameras.	J.5.4
	9		Situation normal – 1.O.R. Killed – 3.O.R. wounded.	J.6.4
	10		Situation normal – 1.O.R. wounded.	J.5.4
	11		Company relieved by 165 M.G. Coy. – March to Camp H.19.	J.6.4
Boesinghe	12		Entrained at POPERINGHE for BOLLEZEELE.	J.5.4
	13		Coy Training – 2/Lieut BEITH reports for duty.	J.4.4
	14-15		Company training.	J.3.4
	16		ROUTE March to ZUTOVE.	J.4.4
Zutove	17		Capt Nichols proceeds on leave – Lieut Stockwell reports from leave.	J.4.4
	19		Lieut Gale proceeds on leave.	J.3.4
	20-29		Company Training – Capt Nichols reports from leave.	J.4.4
	30		Transport moves off to forward areas.	J.3.4

J.S. Hartington Lieut
COMMDG: 164 COY: M.G. CORPS. CAPTAIN

164th MACHINE GUN COMPANY.

WAR DIARY

FOR THE MONTH OF

JULY 1917.

Army Form C. 2118.

July 1917

WAR DIARY
or
INTELLIGENCE SUMMARY.
(Erase heading not required.)

104 Machine Gun Company

Place	Date	Hour	Summary of Events and Information	Remarks and references to Appendices
BRANDHOEK	July 1		Coy marched to LUMBRES - Entrained for BRANDHOEK - Billeted at RED ROSE CAMP 2 O.R. killed & 3 O.R. Wounded.	Winchester 9/H
	July 2		Coy proceeded to relieve 165 Coy M.G.Coy in left 15th Sector taking over the following gun positions.	Winchester 9/H
			ST JEAN - D. Clark 2/Lt Heather. No.1 Section. C 27.3. 4. C 28.1. 3	
	2		POTIJZE - 2/Lt Atkins No 2 Section. C 27.5 C 28.4 C 28.5 L4.1	
			2/Lt Swan " " Section L 3.1	
			CANAL BANK Lt Lockwood 4 Section L8.4 L2.2 L2-3	
			2/Lt Smyth 2/Lt Shute 3 Section in reserve	
			Coy guns at WIELTJE answered SOS on 196 Ch. Y too.	Rabassade 2/M
			Enemy fire on a call heavier to & PLUM FARM - 1250 rds in trouble air craft.	
			Weather rather hazy - Gun position W L 2.3 known to	
			enemy fire on position from enemy Heavies 8in & 5.9. 25 rds on Emergency	H. Ervan ?
	3		Abraham lucky - shelling of CANAL BANK - 17250 rds fired on enemy	
	4		C.T. & back area, declared of shrapnel relief during quiet - 2/Lt Hunt slightly wounded at O 27.5	Winchester 9/H

2353 Wt W2541/1454 700,000 5/15 D. D. & L. A.D.S.S./Forms/C. 2118.

WAR DIARY or INTELLIGENCE SUMMARY

Army Form C. 2118

164 Machine Gun Company

Place	Date	Hour	Summary of Events and Information	Remarks and references to Appendices
LEFT SECTOR	July 5		Heavy artillery bombardment by enemy - shelling in CANAL BANK & ST JEAN with HE & SHRAPNEL	
			2250 Rounds on CALL RESERVE, SQUARE FM & RONDW C24.d	
			2000 rounds on enemy aircraft. B Clark (unnamed on duty) & Pte Beck wounded L/Cpl Taylor W. killed	
	6		Situation continues lively - 2 O.R. killed & 1 O.R. wounded. LA BRIQUE	
			3000 rds on aerial targets. 2250 rds on E.A.	
	7		Situation quieter - 1500 rds on enemy aircraft - 2000 rds on RAT FARM LOW FARM, FREZENBURG X RDS & C - 1500 rds h.f.n. Enter section relief	
			No 4 Section relieved No 2 Sec.	
			" " 2 " " 1	
			" " 1 " " 3	
			" " 3 " " 4	
	8		Relief complete at 1-30 AM. Situation quiet - several enemy planes seen in rear of enemy lines. 3000 rds fired	

(3)

Army Form C. 2118.

164 Machine Gun Company

WAR DIARY
or
INTELLIGENCE SUMMARY.
(Erase heading not required.)

Place	Date	Hour	Summary of Events and Information	Remarks and references to Appendices
LEFT SECTOR	July 9		Situation quiet — C.28.C (WIELTJE) gun emplacement blown in — Ferry in RUPRECHT SQUARE & PLUM FARM	
WIELTJE SECTOR	July 9		FARMS & WIELTJE - ST JULIEN RD. 3000 Rds in all	
	" 10		Situation slightly livelier - 3000 rds fired in RDS, railways in rear of support line	
	" 11		Situation quiet 2/Lt T WILLIAMS (officer reinforcement) reported for duty - 1650 rds on EA	
			machine gun fire in Farms roads tracks & OT defence support line	
			Situation normal — Lieut E Pearce (officer reinforcement) reported for duty	
	" 12		1930 rounds on EA — 3440 rds on CAMBRAI DRIVE PLUM & LOW FARMS & Tramway & Rd	
			E of FRIEDENBERG Eveningen developed although with very heavy bombardment	
			of CANAL BANK & YPRES — several dumps fired & 3 hangars (4-5) just out of	
	13th	1 AM	ST Melting in talley opposite Ch g sy Hg Ct Melting in (our officers) + CSM Bayly &	
			wounded by shell from exploded magazine opposite — extensive damage to	
			dump on CANAL BANK. Gun details by survivors ? Orla + 20 other workers to	
			hospital suffering from effects of gas	
			1275 rds fired EA 3250 on tracks & samways tulung enemy wiring parties	
	14th		Situation quieter Capt NICHOLS & Lts trink & Lepine (reinforcements)	

Army Form C. 2118.

(4)

164 Oberhalm Gun Company

WAR DIARY
or
INTELLIGENCE SUMMARY.

(Erase heading not required.)

Place	Date	Hour	Summary of Events and Information	Remarks and references to Appendices
WIELTJE SECTOR	July 14		2/Lt Clark took over command of company – 1500 rds in trench behind SQUARE FM & tramway in rear of FRIEZENBERG. 630 rds in M.E.A. Further enemy trenches at night – gas shells from enemy at night.	Appendix 5¼
	15		2250 RDS in farm & roads – 970 rds on enemy cn emp – trench bdwn xroads neighbourhood of CANAL BANK.	Nil. Weather Sd.
	16		2250 rds in WIELTJE – ST JULIEN – WIELTJE – GRAVENSTAFEL RDS from Vnsepervill/	Appendix 6½
	17		750 Rds on enemy emerg. Enemy employ gas shells against practically whole sector. Commencement of heavy bombdmt of trenches fire – 43000 rds fired.	Nil.
	18		Continuation of above – 66,500 rds fired. Other casualties at 8th G. Coy of 18 reinforcements.	Nil.
	19		Evacuation of wounded. S.T. 67,500 23 OR. reinforcements.	
	20		Indices be extended. Relief of Coy (less POT/JZE = section by 166 MG Coy. Bapmakeast Derby Camp.	
Derbyleings	20		Derby Camp – Cleaning of Arms etc.	
	22		POTIJZE SECTOR. Relieved by 165 MG Coy. Coy moved to WATOU (due 3 others) arrival W REST CAMP at 6.30 PM. Capt Oberhin joined Company from hospital.	
	23		S/Lt Thomson (2nd in command) 2/Lt Lomes & Hayden joined Coy. 2/Lt Doughe injured Coy Army.	

Army Form C. 2118.

WAR DIARY
or
INTELLIGENCE SUMMARY.
(Erase heading not required.)

164 Machine Gun Company   5

Instructions regarding War Diaries and Intelligence Summaries are contained in F. S. Regs., Part II. and the Staff Manual respectively. Title pages will be prepared in manuscript.

Place	Date	Hour	Summary of Events and Information	Remarks and references to Appendices
REST CAMP	July 25		Coy training - 2/Lt T. Martin joined Coy. Coy presented by rifle rack.	R.T
			to BRAND + OSH (QUERY CAMP)	
QUERY CAMP	26		Training & preparations for trenches	R.T
	27		" " "	R.T
	28		W Day — do —	R.T
	29		X " — do —	R.T
	30		Y " — do —	R.T
	31		Z Day. Zero hour was 3·50 am. 3 No.3 section under Lt. Stockwell & Brown moved off from No. 4 section.	R.T
DIV'L SECTOR			N.4 section under Lt. Stockwell & Brown moved off from the positions about 2 hours to minute after Zero & reached the GREENLINE about Z+8 hours. The enemy counter-attacked about Z+5 hrs. 3 After covering the withdrawal of our infantry, who had possession of No.3 & 4 section also withdraw to the earlier to do so No.3 & 4 sections consolidated on that position. Lt Brown was wounded & is believed to be a prisoner.	R.T

Army Form C. 2118.

WAR DIARY
or
INTELLIGENCE SUMMARY.

(Erase heading not required.)

16.4 N.F. Coy

Instructions regarding War Diaries and Intelligence Summaries are contained in F. S. Regs., Part II. and the Staff Manual respectively. Title pages will be prepared in manuscript.

Place	Date	Hour	Summary of Events and Information	Remarks and references to Appendices
Oppy Sect	31		Zero. Nos 1 & 2 sections under Lt CLARK and 2Lt ALDOUS moved forward from their assembly position at OPPY at ZERO + 5h. 20 minutes. Field made was bad. No 1 section began mopping the high ground S of GAVRELLE and No 2 taken acquired strong point shelter in the TRAM lines. No 1 Section on right and No 2 Section on left held up by the counter attacks for one time but eventually succeeded. Both sections constructed in the BLACK LINE	

R Thomas Cy
Lieut
No 1 16 Y
3/11/17

SECRET.   Copy No. 1.

164th MACHINE GUN COMPANY ORDER No. 126.

Ref. Maps: ST. JULIEN. 28. N.W.2. Ed. 6A. 1/10,000.
            ZONNEBEKE,   28. N.W.2. Ed. 6A. 1/10,000.
                                                26th July, 1917.
----

1.   On 'Z' day the 55th Division (Left Division, XIX Corps) will take part in a general attack of the Fifth Army in conjunction with Second Army and First French Army.

        The 15th Division is attacking on the right, and the 39th Division (Right Division of XVIII Corps) is attacking on the left.

2.   It is the intention

        (a) with the object of preparing for a further advance, to capture and occupy as a line of resistance the enemy's GHELUVELT-LANGEMARCK Line, and to throw out strong outposts to obtain a footing on the GRAVENSTAFEL SPUR and occupy enemy works to the East of the GHELUVELT-LANGEMARCK Line as far as about the line TORONTO-AVIATIK FARM.

        (b) In the event of the enemy evacuating the GRAVENSTAFEL SWITCH and the ZONNEBEKE-STADEN Line, to push forward the line of resistance, in touch with the 15th Division on our right, to the GRAVENSTAFEL SPUR with the same object as in (a).

        It is not the intention to attack any position in which the enemy shows resistance beyond the objectives defined in (a) above.

3.   The Brigade will be in position on the CONGREVE WALK-LIVERPOOL TRENCH Line by 2 a.m. on 'Z' day. Orders for move of the Brigade to this line from the concentration area are being issued separately.

4.   Guns and ammunition will be sent to M.G. Section Headquarters, ST. JEAN, by limber on 'Y' day. Sections will collect these on the way up to assembly positions on morning of 'Z' day.

        Sections will proceed to assembly positions as follows:-

        Nos. 1 and 2 Sections under Lieut. Clark, together with 16 pack animals (8 with gun carriers and 8 with S.A.A. box carriers) will be in position at I.3.a. by ZERO plus 4 hrs. Details as per instructions already issued.

        No. 3 Section under Lieut. Pearce will be in position with 1/4th N. Lancs. R. in BIRCH WALK-CONGREVE WAK Line by 2 a.m. on 'Z' day. Arrival of Section to be reported to O.C. 1/4th N. Lancs. R. personally by O.C. Section. Details as per instructions already issued.

        No. 4 Section under Lieut. Stockwell will be in position with 2/5th Lancs. Fus. in CONGREVE WALK-LIVERPOOL TRENCH Line by 2 a.m. on 'Z' day. Arrival of Section to be reported to O.C. 2/5th Lancs. Fus. personally by O.C. Section. Details as per instructions already issued.

5.	The attack will be carried out in three stages as under:-

1st Objective. At ZERO 165th Infantry Brigade on the right and 166th Infantry Brigade on the left will capture and consolidate the enemy front system of trenches up to, and including, the BLUE Line.

2nd Objective. At ZERO plus 1 hr. 15 mins. 165th and 166th Infantry Brigades will capture and consolidate the enemy's second line system (STUTZPUNKT LINE) up to, and including, the BLACK Line.
	At ZERO plus 3 hrs. 53 mins. 166th Infantry Brigade will advance their left to the dotted GREEN Line.

3rd Objective.
	(a) At ZERO plus 6 hrs. 20 mins. the 164th Infantry Brigade will pass through the 165th and 166th Infantry Brigades, will on the BLACK Line, will capture and consolidate the enemy's third line system (GHELUVELT-LANGEMARCK LINE) up to, and including, the GREEN Line, and will at the same time push forward posts to about the line TORONTO-AVIATIK FARM
	(b) In the event of the enemy having evacuated the GRAVENSTAFEL SWITCH AND THE ZONNEBEKE-STADEN Line, 164th Infantry Brigade, after the protective barrage in front of the GREEN Line ceases at ZERO plus 8 hrs. 20 mins., will establish a line of resistance along the GRAVENSTAFEL SPUR, in touch on the right about GRAVENSTAFEL with the 15th Division, and on the left with 39th Division on GREEN Line.

	Until the 1st and 2nd objectives are taken, the Brigade will be in reserve.

6.	At ZERO plus 4 hrs. 40 mins. Nos. 3 and 4 Sections will advance (manhandling guns, etc.) with their respective Battalions subject to orders of O.C. Battalions. Advance to the BLACK Line will be in teams at 50 yards. interval. After leaving the BLACK Line, and on deployment of Battalions, the teams of each Section will proceed behind the rear wave of the attack, but the method of advance from this point will be left in the hands of O.C. Sections. In view of the fact that the work of the guns will not commence under normal circumstances until the GREEN Line is taken, it becomes the responsibility of Section Commanders to take every precaution possible to protect their teams from enemy barrage, etc. whilst the advance is in progress, so that when called upon by O.C. Battalions to take up their positions in Strong Points in BLACK DOTTED Line, they will at once be able to do so. Under these circumstances teams will not enter the GREEN Line until same has been captured and mopped up. The teams will take cover in shell holes approximately 300 yards in rear of same. During the advance to the GREEN Line O.C. Sections will keep in closest touch with O.C. Battalions.

	On arrival at the GREEN Line O.C. Sections will at once get into touch with O.C. Companies who are furnishing platoons to occupy the Strong Points in the BLACK DOTTED Line. Approximate positions of these points and proposed siting of machine guns in accordance with previous instructions issued. When once in these points the object of the machine guns is
	(a) To hold them at all costs;
	(b) Harass the enemy with direct fire whenever possible, with particular reference to the Valley of the HANEBEEKE, ABRAHAM HEIGHTS and the PASSCHENDAELE RIDGE.

The left gun of No. 4 Section will cover the front of the 39th Division on the left, and the right gun of No. 3 Section will cover the front of the 15th Division on the right. Section Commanders should eadeavour at the earliest moment to establish laiason with machine guns of these Divisions for purposes of co-operation.

7. Nos. 1 and 2 Sections under the command of Lieut. Clark will remain in their positions at I.3.a. until the Right Rear Battalion moves forward. They will then move forward, with pack animals if possible, to the high ground S. of GALLIPOLI (approximately D.19.b.31.70)

4 guns will on arrival at this point immediately dig in and prepare for opening direct overhead fire supporting the attack on GRAVENSTAFEL SPUR, and in addition will enfilade KANSAS CROSS-GRAVENSTAFEL ROAD in order to protect the right flank of the Brigade.

The remaining 4 guns will proceed under 2/Lieut. Aldous to a position behind the crest S. of SOMME (approximately D.13.c.40.40) They will at once dig in and await orders to occupy Strong Points 4, 5, 6 and 7, approximate positions of which are as follows:

    4 = D.7.d.05.50.
    5 = D.7.d.00.15.
    6 = D.13.b.75.00.
    7 = D.14.c.55.30.

1/8th Liverpool R. are furnishing an Infantry Garrison for these Points as soon as constructed by R.E.'s. 2/Lieut. Aldous will therefore report his location to O.C. 1/8th Liverpool R.

8. Ammunition.

Lieut. Clark before leaving his Assembly Position will detail 2/Lieut. Williams as O.C. Ammunition Dump. The duty of this Officer will be
(a) Take over the 8 pack animals belonging to Nos. 3 and 4 Sections
(b) As soon as possible move the dump from I.3.a. up to a position near the Brigade Forward Dump, which will be formed approximately at D.13.c.30.80.
(c) He will detail Corporal Anderson and 8 men to go forward with the first load. Cpl. Anderson will be in charge of this forward dump and the men will be used for carrying ammunition as required to the Sections. When the ammunition is all up to the forward dump, 2/Lieut. Williams will himself move up and get into touch with 2/Lieut. Carberry, O.C. Brigade Dump. The pack animals will remain at I.3.a. under L/Cpl. Jones until further orders.

Section Officers if requiring ammunition will send a runner to the forward dump. O.C. Dump will immediately send up a carrying party of 3 men to 2 boxes of ammunition under the guidance of the Section Runner.

9. Water.

In addition to the 1 Petron Tin per team which is being carried a further supply will be available at the forward ammunition dump.

10. Headquarters.

The Advanced Headquarters of O.C. Company will be in the mined dug-out at WIELTJE with Brigade Headquarters, where all messages will be sent. Should these Headquarters be moved forward during 'Z' day Sections will at once be advised.

11. Communications.

It is of the utmost improtance that messages be sent back to Headquarters immediately a Sections' guns are in position. Rough maps showing approximate positions, direction and field of fire of guns are of the greatest value. It is obvious too that any further information such as location or movement of the enemy should be immediately sent to Headquarters for transmission to Brigade.

12. Regimental Aid Posts (At ZERO hour).

164th Infantry Brigade (in support):

I. 4. a. 8. 3.
I. 4. a. 8. 4.

Collecting posts will be situated at
C. 27. d. 3. L.   JUNCTION ROAD.
I. 4. a. 7. 3.   POTIJZE.

13. Enemy Maps, Documents, etc.

Any enemy maps or documents found in dug-outs or other places should be placed in sand-bags and sent immediately to Headquarters marked "Enemy Documents- Urgent." Severest disciplinary action will be taken against any N.C.O. or man found souvenir hunting. All ranks are reminded of previous warnings as to enemy 'booby traps' and all reasonable precautions must be taken against such devices.

14.   Administrative Arrangements are per instructions already issued.

15.   ACKNOWLEDGE.

                                                             Capt.
Cmdg. 164th Machine Gun Company.

Copy No. 1 - File.   No. 7 - 2/5th Lancs. Fus.
        2 - War Diary.   8 - Division M.G. Officer.
        3 - 164th Infantry Brigade.   9 - Lieut. Clark.
        4 - 1/4th R. Lancs. R.   10 - 2/Lt. Aldous.
        5 - 1/8th Liverpool R.   11 - Lieut. Pearce.
        6 - 1/4th N. Lancs. R.   12 - Lieut. Stockwell.

Vol 19

CONFIDENTIAL

WAR DIARY

of

164TH MACHINE GUN COY

AUGUST 1917

Army Form C. 2118.

WAR DIARY
or
INTELLIGENCE SUMMARY.
(Erase heading not required.)

August 1917

Place	Date	Hour	Summary of Events and Information	Remarks and references to Appendices
In the line Div sector	31/7/17		No 1 Section attached to B Coys P.? "2 " " " " F " " "3 " " " " E Coy P? "4 " " " " H " N Lewis P? 25 Lewis Gun.	P.T.
			The Company [illegible] met the Bnde in an assembly area near the WIELTJE line.	
			Stealthily crossing the BLUE LINE & then the BLACK LINE the went up to the Bde. & [illegible] to attack to the GREEN LINE.	
			The [illegible] of the line were :-	
			BLACK — WINE HOUSE — POMMERN REDTE	
			GREEN — WORST FARM — KULL — KANSAS CROSS — ANZAC — ZONNEBEKE RD	
			The section with their respective Battalions [illegible] their position [illegible] the GREEN LINE about 7.00 A.M. from [illegible] position, this were [illegible] — attack by the enemy & compelled to withdraw to the BLACK LINE where they dug in	

Army Form C. 2118.

WAR DIARY
or
INTELLIGENCE SUMMARY
(Erase heading not required.)

Army 1917
16th M.T.

Place	Date	Hour	Summary of Events and Information	Remarks and references to Appendices
DMLT SECTION	1/8/17		3 Reinforcements. Nos 1,2,3 Sections were reported to Bde H.Q. at BILGE TRENCH. No 4 Section was retained on duty at Bde H.Q.	P.T.
	2/8/17		The Coy was ordered to be ready to move to M.T. DERRY CAMP. Bn crossed the open field.	
			Moving the opposed field. 21 hours under Shrapnel shrouded at 7 p.m. Casualties at 1 a.m. Company moved off R.A. H.Q's M.T. line begun. C.O. N. CEBUS. B. reported to B Coy & remained to H.Q. Klein Pebbles.	R.T.
	3/8/17		Cleaning & fitting up material. Training.	R.T.
	4/8/17			R.T.
	5/8/17		Marched to BEZZIE where Bn was entrained. Detrained at NOYELLES then by motor bus to HOLM FORT.	R.T.
	6/8/17		Training.	R.T.

WAR DIARY or INTELLIGENCE SUMMARY.

Army Form C. 2118.

August 1917

Instructions regarding War Diaries and Intelligence Summaries are contained in F. S. Regs., Part II. and the Staff Manual respectively. Title pages will be prepared in manuscript.

(Erase heading not required.)

Place	Date	Hour	Summary of Events and Information	Remarks and references to Appendices
NIEUPORT	7/8		France - 25 O.R. reinforcements	R.T.
	8		Trenches	R.T.
	9		MAJOR C.H.K. CRAWFORD (R.A.M.C. attd.) [illegible] for gas poisoning & [illegible]	R.T.
	10		Trenches	R.T.
			"	R.T.
	11		" 1 O.R. reinforcement	R.T.
	12		Shermo barrage	R.T.
	13		Trenches ne Harms been [illegible] [illegible] R.E. [illegible] Engineers	R.T.
	14		N.J. [illegible] on ENEMY [illegible] [illegible] [illegible] 2 O.R.s and [illegible]	R.T.
			Lt. THOMSON [illegible] by [illegible]	R.T.
	15		Trenches - [illegible] to attack on NIEUPORT	R.T.
			[illegible] [illegible] plans for [illegible] [illegible] [illegible] [illegible]	R.T.
			Lt. WADDINGTON [illegible] [illegible] [illegible] 2 O.R. reinforcements [illegible] the Bn.	
	16		Trenches - Relieved [illegible] [illegible] NIEUPORT	R.T.
	17		" - March to YPRES	R.T.
	18		Trenches - Batt. Rest [illegible] 2 batteries of [illegible] [illegible] N.I [illegible] on ENEMY [illegible]	R.T.

A7092. Wt. W12639/M1295 750,000. 1/17. D. D & L., Ltd. Forms/C2118/14.

Army Form C. 2118.

WAR DIARY
INTELLIGENCE SUMMARY

(Erase heading not required.)

Instructions regarding War Diaries and Intelligence Summaries are contained in F. S. Regs., Part II. and the Staff Manual respectively. Title pages will be prepared in manuscript.

August 1917 ..... 16th M.G. Coy.

Place	Date	Hour	Summary of Events and Information	Remarks and references to Appendices
ALDER FORT	19		Church parade.	P.T.
	20		Training — Indoor scheme — Noisy section firing on CHEMIC RANGE	R.T.
	21		Training — Use of Oxy. Bil apptk.	P.T.
	22		" — "Defence of a post"	P.T.
	23		D. — Section parade	P.T.
	24		D. — Lt THOMSON returned from leave	P.T.
	25		D. — Inspection of trans. Gun Officer by Brook Jun N.C.O.	P.T.
	26		Church parade	P.T.
	27		Training — Barrage drill — Lt ELMONDSTON inspected ger det	P.T.
	28		D. — Section parade — L/Cpl CARR promoted to Cpl to U.S.	P.T.
	29		D. — Tactical scheme. No 1 Section on "B" Range. M.G. on CLASS RANGE	P.T.
	30		D. Training — Gun & Barrage drill	P.T.
	31		D. — Tactical exercise	P.T.

R Thomson Lt for Major
M.G. Coy

164th M.G. Coy

War Diary
for the month of
September 1917

30 Sep 1917

164th M.G. Coy. Army Form C. 2118.

Sheet 1.

SEPTEMBER, 1917. WAR DIARY or INTELLIGENCE SUMMARY.

(Erase heading not required.)

Instructions regarding War Diaries and Intelligence Summaries are contained in F.S. Regs., Part II, and the Staff Manual respectively. Title pages will be prepared in manuscript.

Place	Date	Hour	Summary of Events and Information	Remarks and references to Appendices
AUDENFORT	SEPT. 1.		Coy. Training. - Barrage and Gun Drill.	R.T.
"	2.		Church Parade.	R.T.
"	3.		Coy. Training - Tactical problems. - No.4 Section attached to 2/5 Lan. Fus.	R.T.
"	4.		Coy. Training - Barrage and Gun Drill	R.T.
"	5.		Brigade Tactical exercise near RONVILLE.	R.T.
"	6.		Coy. Training - Divisional Horse Show near NORDAUSQUES.	R.T.
"	7.		Coy. Training - Gun Drill.	R.T.
"	8.		Coy. Training - Gun Drill.	R.T.
"	9.		Church Parade	R.T.
			Presentation of decorations by Brigadier General C.I. Stockwell, D.S.O. at AUDREHEM. The undermentioned received decorations	R.T.
			43203 Sgt. Baldock. L. M.M.	R.T.
			26153 L/c. Martin. W. D.C.M.	R.T.
			45847 Pte. Hawkins. N. M.M.	R.T.
			53653 " Earl J.D. M.M.	R.T.
			44547 " McMahon. N. M.M.	R.T.

Army Form C. 2118.

Page 2.   164 MACHINE GUN COY

SEPTEMBER 1917. WAR DIARY
or
INTELLIGENCE SUMMARY.

(Erase heading not required.)

Place	Date	Hour	Summary of Events and Information	Remarks and references to Appendices
AUDENFURT	Sept 9		The undermentioned officer and N.C.O. have also been awarded decorations.	P.T.
			Lieut. G.E.R CLARK. – Military Cross.	P.T.
			22521. Sgt. F. LORD – D.C.M.	P.T.
	10		Divisional tactical scheme near RONVILLE.	P.T.
"	11		Training	P.T.
"	12		Coy training. Transport move to NORDAUSQUES.	P.T.
"	13		Train loading party of 100 men proceeded to AUDRUICQ. Remainder of Company preparing to move.	P.T.
"	14	6.a.m.	Company proceeded by route march to AUDRUICQ.	P.T.
		1.30 p.m.	Entrained at AUDRUICQ, and detrained at PESELHOEK (POPERINGHE) then marched to camp at GOLDFISH CHATEAU, arriving in Camp at	P.T.
GOLDFISH CHATEAU (YPRES NORTH AREA.)	15	2.a.m.	2.a.m.	P.T.
			Coy Training	P.T.
	16		Church Parade – enemy aircraft bombed camp – 1 O.R. died of wounds and 1 O.R. w.d.d.	P.T.

Army Form C. 2118.

WAR DIARY
or
INTELLIGENCE SUMMARY.
(Erase heading not required.)

Page 3.

164 Machine Gun Coy.

Instructions regarding War Diaries and Intelligence Summaries are contained in F. S. Regs., Part II. and the Staff Manual respectively. Title pages will be prepared in manuscript.

September '17

Place	Date	Hour	Summary of Events and Information	Remarks and references to Appendices
Goldfish Chateau	Sep. 17.		Preparations for Trenches.	P.7.
Wieltje		7.45 p.m	Battle portion of Company marched up to the line. Advanced Company Headquarters were established at WIELTJE mined dugout. "B" team personnel proceeded to Coy. Transport Lines at G.5.c.7.3. (Ref. map BELGIUM 28 N.W.)	P.7. P.7.
"	17-24.		See attached narrative maps - Appendix I. Congratulatory messages have been received from the Secretary of State for War, the Commander in Chief (through V Corps) Fifth Army Commander, Second Army Commander, V Corps Commander, Major General Commanding 55th Division, and West Lancs Reserve Brigade - Appendix II.	P.7. P.7.
Vlamertinghe	"	4 a.m	Coy returned to camp at VLAMERTINGHE.	
	24.	3 p.m	Company entrained at VLAMERTINGHE and detrained at POPERINGHE, proceeding from there to the Ferme des Trappistes (WATOU AREA) by motor Lorries, arriving there at 6 p.m.	P.7. P.7.
Watou Area	25.	6 p.m	Marched from WATOU AREA to HOPOUTRE STATION (POPERINGHE) and entrained there for BAPAUME.	P.7.

Army Form C. 2118.

WAR DIARY
or
INTELLIGENCE SUMMARY.
(Erase heading not required.)

Page 4.

—164 MACHINE GUN COMPANY

Instructions regarding War Diaries and Intelligence SEPTEMBER 1917
Summaries are contained in F. S. Regs., Part II.
and the Staff Manual respectively. Title pages
will be prepared in manuscript.

Place	Date 1917 SEPT.	Hour	Summary of Events and Information	Remarks and references to Appendices
BAPAUME	26	4.30 p.m.	Arrived at BAPAUME at 4.30 p.m. detraining there. Company marched to camp on YPRES-ETRICOURT ROAD, arriving there at 9.40 p.m	P.T.
LECHELLE	27	9.40. 12 noon	Company marched to new camp at LECHELLE, taking over from 17th M.G.Coy.	P.T.
"	28		Company training - Cleaning guns & and overhauling kit and equipment.	P.T.
"	29		Gun cleaning - Company training.	P.T.
"	30		Church Parades - Inspection of Camp by the C.O.	P.T.

J. Crawford
Major
O.C. 164th Machine Gun Coy.

POSITION of GUNS — 21.9.17

1:10 000 K.3. EDITION I. Parts of { 28 N.E. / 28 N.W. }

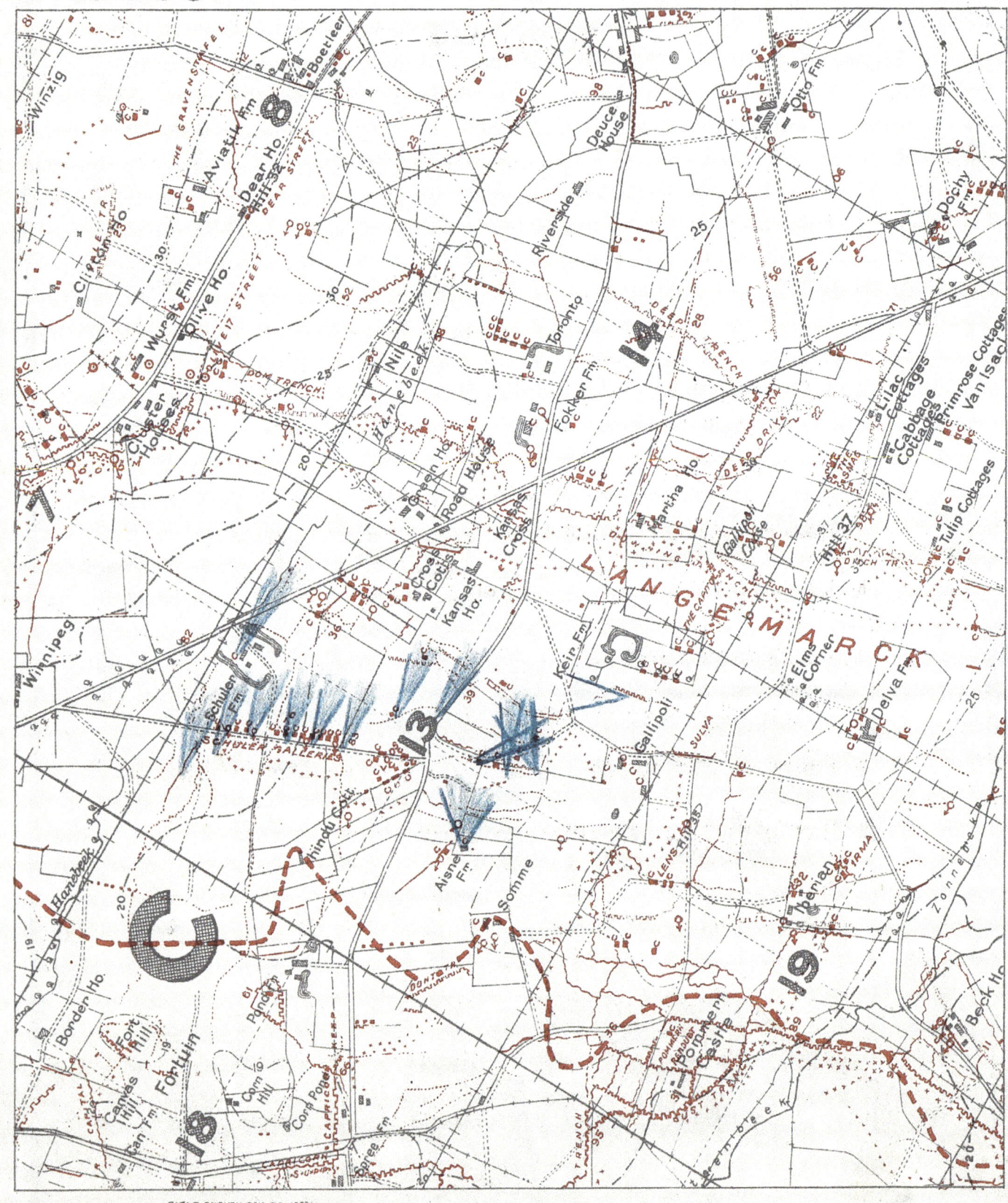

Message Form.

..................Division.

Map reference or mark own position on Map at back.

1. I am at..

2. I am at..and am consolidating.

3. I am at..and have consolidated.

4. I need :—Ammunition.
    Bombs.
    Rifle Grenades.
    Water.
    Very lights.
    Stokes shells.

5. Enemy forming up for counter-attack at..

6. I am in touch with........................... on $\begin{matrix}\text{Right}\\\text{Left}\end{matrix}$ at...............................

7. I am not in touch on $\begin{matrix}\text{Right}\\\text{Left}\end{matrix}$

8. Am being shelled from..

9. I estimate my present strength at ....rifles.

10. Hostile $\begin{Bmatrix}\text{Battery}\\\text{Machine Gun}\\\text{Trench Mortar}\end{Bmatrix}$ active at...

Time........................a.m. (p.m.)   Name..

Date..   Platoon................. Company..............

Place..   Battalion..

POSITIONS OF GUNS — 20.9.17

1:10 000 K.3. EDITION I. Parts of { 28 N.E. / 28 N.W.

Scale: 1:10,000.

Message Form.

........................Division.

Map reference or mark own position on Map at back.

1. I am at...

2. I am at...and am consolidating.

3. I am at...and have consolidated.

4. I need :—Ammunition.
   Bombs.
   Rifle Grenades.
   Water.
   Very lights.
   Stokes shells.

5. Enemy forming up for counter-attack at...

6. I am in touch with........................... on Right / Left at ....

7. I am not in touch on Right / Left

8. Am being shelled from...

9. I estimate my present strength at ....rifles.

10. Hostile { Battery / Machine Gun / Trench Mortar } active at...

Time......................a.m. (p.m.)　　Name..

Date..　　Platoon................. Company...........

Place...　　Battalion..

Positions of Guns 22.9.17

NOTE.
S.A.A. Dumps.

Pond Farm	112 belt boxes	20,000 S.A.A.
Somme	65 do.	10,000 S.A.A.
Fort Hill	28 do.	10,000 S.A.A.
Schuler Galleries	30 do.	4,000 S.A.A.

D.13.d.1.5. – 20,000. GERMAN. 15,000 used.

1:10 000 **K.3.** **EDITION 1.** Parts of { 28 N.E. / 28 N.W.

FIELD SURVEY COY. R.E. (253/) 16·9·17
Scale. 1:10,000.

Message Form.

.....................Division.

Map reference or mark own position on Map at back.

1. I am at..

2. I am at..and am consolidating.

3. I am at..and have consolidated.

4. I need :—Ammunition.
    Bombs.
    Rifle Grenades.
    Water.
    Very lights.
    Stokes shells.

5. Enemy forming up for counter-attack at...

6. I am in touch with............................. on Right/Left at..

7. I am not in touch on Right/Left.

8. Am being shelled from...

9. I estimate my present strength at ....rifles.

10. Hostile { Battery / Machine Gun / Trench Mortar } active at..

Time............................a.m. (p.m.)   Name..

Date..   Platoon.................. Company...........

Place..   Battalion..

APPENDIX I

164th MACHINE GUN COMPANY.

Report by Officer Commanding on operations from
18th to 24th September, 1917.

At 8 p.m. on the night of the 17th inst. I marched the Company from the NORTH YPRES Area to dug-outs in CAMBRAI TRENCH, arriving there about 10.30 p.m. After seeing the Company settled and guns and ammunition placed under cover, I reconnoitred the ground for advanced Machine Gun Dumps and approaches to assembly positions, returning at 6 a.m. on the 18th inst. During the day we were heavily shelled, and about 6 p.m. two of our guns, which were under cover in a dug-out, received a direct hit putting them out of action. I immediately wired for two new guns, which were received the following day. At 8.30 p.m. eight guns and their teams moved off to relieve the 166th Machine Gun Company, two (2) guns taking up their positions in POND FARM, six (6) in CALL RESERVE and two (2) in JEW HILL, the relief being completed about 11.30 p.m.

On the morning of the 19th inst. at 5 a.m., after a very heavy shelling, one of the guns at JEW HILL was blown up by a direct hit, and was replaced at once by one of the reserve guns, and another gun was obtained from Ordnance. During the night of the 19/20 I had carrying parties from the Sections and formed advanced dumps of ammunition and belt boxes at SOMME, POND FARM and FORT HILL.

The Company moved to the assembly positions the same night, arriving there by midnight, the sections attaching themselves to their respective Battalions as follows:-

No. 1 Section attached to the 1/4th R. Lancs. R.
No. 4 Section and 2 guns of No. 2 Section to 2/5th Lancs. Fus.
The remaining 2 guns of No. 2 Section to 1/8th Liverpool R.
No. 3 Section to 1/4th N. Lancs. R.

Company Headquarters were established at WIELTJE MINE DUG-OUT.

At ZERO hour on the 20th inst. our Artillery opened their creeping barrage and the Infantry moved forward to the attack, the Machine Gun Sections moving forward with Battalion Headquarters. During the day I received messages that the guns had taken up positions shown on the attached map. On the 21st inst. about 6.30 p.m. I went out to reconnoitre the gun position at AISNE FARM, but was caught by the enemy's barrage and got blown into a shell hole and was rendered unconscious. After recovering I returned to Headquarters. Some of my guns had moved forward during the day and occupied positions as shown on attached map for the 21st inst. An enemy counter attack was launched about 7 p.m. and all available guns were turned on, completely breaking up the attack, the enemy being mown down by our machine gun fire. On the 22nd inst. our guns helped to repel an enemy counter attack on HILL 37. On the night of the 23/24 the Company was relieved by the 174th Machine Gun Company and I reported relief complete by 1.30 a.m. and marched the Company back to billets at VLAMERTINGHE.

1.

2.

NOTES.

Approximate positions of guns to be taken up, when positions were consolidated, were sent to Os.C. Battalions on the night of the 19th inst.

The arrangements for forward ammunition dumps, proved most satisfactory as it curtailed the number of carriers required from Battalions, and the guns had always sufficient ammunition to repel any counter attacks.

Good use was made of captured enemy machine guns in repelling counter attacks and husbanding our ammunition.

I consider that the excellent work done by the Company, was materially helped by the close co-operation of the Os.C. Battalions and Company Officers. Good assistance in belt filling was rendered by the infantry.

The employment of slings for carrying guns and belt boxes, which were made for this purpose by the Company, proved most successful during the operations.

Major.
Cmdg. 164th Machine Gun Company.

28.9.17.

164th MACHINE GUN COMPANY.

APPENDIX II.

The following congratulatory telegrams were received by the 55th (West Lancashire) Division:—

"The Commander-in-Chief visited Corps H. Qrs. this evening and expressed himself very pleased in the work of both Divisions and sends them his congratulations and thanks."

"Fifth Army wire begins aaa Please congratulate 55th Division on the gallant defence of HILL 37 yesterday and upon the energy and resource displayed by Commanders on the spot in organising counter attacks aaa Ends aaa."

"Fifth Army wire begins aaa The Army Commander wishes to thank all arms and all ranks for their splendid efforts in to-day's battle aaa Co-operation between Infantry, Artillery and Flying Corps has been excellent and very important successes have been gained all along the front aaa Ends aaa

"Corps Commander thanks Field and Heavy Artillery for their good work and the F.O.Os. for the very useful and timely information sent in aaa Ends aaa

"Corps Commander congratulates 9th and 55th Divisions and thanks them for their success to-day aaa Ends aaa

"55th Division. Please convey to all ranks 55th Division the Army Commander's congratulations on the fine record of the Division during the hard fighting of the past two months aaa The Army Commander wishes specially to thank all ranks for their splendid efforts which have contributed greatly to the success of the last attack and to wish them all good luck and success in the future despite their long period in the line prior to commencement of operations they have well maintained and increased their high reputation.
FIFTH ARMY."

"G.O.C. 55th Division, FRANCE. Brigadier General STUART and all ranks West Lancashire Reserve Brigade send heartiest congratulations to West Lancashire Division on their splendid success."

From GENERAL SIR HERBERT PLUMER, G.C.M.G., G.C.V.O., K.C.B., commanding the 2nd Army:—
"GENERAL JEUDWINE, Commanding 55th Division.
Many congratulations to you and your Division on your success yesterday aaa You must have accounted for a great many.
GENERAL PLUMER."

From The Right Honourable E.G.V. Earl of DERBY, K.G., G.C.V.O., C.B., Secretary of State for War:—
"GENERAL JEUDWINE, 55th Division Hdqrs., B.E.F.
Well done 55th Division accept my most hearty congratulations
I sincerely trust your losses are not heavy.
DERBY."

The Major General Commanding wishes to add his thanks and congratulations to all arms and ranks of the Division.

There is no doubt whatever that in addition to making a very substantial advance over difficult ground stubbornly defended, well organised, and liberally provided with strong cover, artillery, and machine guns, the Division, aided most ably by the Corps Heavy Artillery, succeeded in dealing the enemy a very heavy blow, and causing him severe losses.

Success was due to the fine determination shown by all ranks and the hearty co-operation of Artillery, Engineers, Infantry, Machine Gun Companies, Trench Mortars and R.A.M.C. with each other, which is the sign of a united and disciplined Division.

Wm Denny
164 McKinley
Chicago

164 M.G. Coy

Army Form C. 2118.

WAR DIARY
or
INTELLIGENCE SUMMARY.
(Erase heading not required.)

Instructions regarding War Diaries and Intelligence Summaries are contained in F. S. Regs., Part II. and the Staff Manual respectively. Title pages will be prepared in manuscript.

Place	Date	Hour	Summary of Events and Information	Remarks and references to Appendices
LECHELLE	Oct 1st		Coy Training - Squad Drill Gas Drill Clamming & Gas Sentry Posts	Appendix
"	Oct 2		Coy Training - Range Drill	Appendix
"	Oct 3	10 am	Coy marched off to AIZECOURT LE BAS via ETRICOURT, MANANCOURT and NURLU. Entrainment of Coy transport at MANANCOURT by Lieut Grenville who took over El CO of the remainder of the transport Company	
"		1.45	under Lieuts Grenves at AIZECOURT LE BAS. Arrived there at 1.45 pm	
AIZECOURT LE BAS	Oct 4		2nd Lt Owen proceeded on leave to UK	Appendix
"			Coy training - Stalking & approach to Action - Squad Drill Gun Drill	Appendix
"			2nd Lieutenant Overland Cluwan Joined	Appendix
"	Oct 5		Coy training Squad Drill, Gun Drill, W/d Drill at AIZECOURT LE BAS	Appendix
"	Oct 6		Coy training Section Parades Harnessing of horses, Gas instruction	Appendix
"	Oct 7		Church Parade	
"	Oct 8		Change of Billets to make room for Canadians. HQ Cookhouse & H Section line amended to fit in. Coy Lecture by Captain Shingleton General St Quintin	Appendix
"	Oct 9		Coy/See training Gas instruction Aeroplane Co-operation of horse by 5th Airmys Letters on Lovat Scouts	Appendix
"	Oct 10		Coy/See Parade Section Officer	Appendix

Army Form C. 2118.

WAR DIARY
or
INTELLIGENCE SUMMARY.
(Erase heading not required.)

Instructions regarding War Diaries and Intelligence Summaries are contained in F. S. Regs., Part II. and the Staff Manual respectively. Title pages will be prepared in manuscript.

Place	Date	Hour	Summary of Events and Information	Remarks and references to Appendices
AIZECOURT LE BAS	Oct 10th		[illegible]	
	11th		Reconnaissance of lines by Section Officers	
LEMPIRE	12th		Recce at 10.5 MG Coy in LEMPIRE sector. Relief complete 6.0 p.m.	
SECTOR			No 4 Section with 2nd Lt Smith. No 1 Section with 2nd Lt [illegible] No 2 Section in reserve under 2nd Lt Hutton	
	13th		[illegible] movement from 1000 to 1500 to lead from two Boches at ALLE [illegible]	
	14th		Shoots carried out between returned from leave 3.50 a.m. onwards on CLERMONT FARM, CROSS ROADS & BONY VILLAGE 3500 [illegible] CROSS ROADS at Nil. 21 & 22 526.3+1 GILLEMONT FARM, MACQUINCOURT VALLEY	
	15th			
	16th		2nd Lt [illegible] [illegible] BONY & 500 rounds Road between AU 926 [illegible]	
	17th		10.30 a.m. on [illegible] LEMPIRE [illegible] 4500 [illegible]	

Army Form C. 2118.

104 M.G. Coy
3

WAR DIARY
or
INTELLIGENCE SUMMARY.
(Erase heading not required.)

Instructions regarding War Diaries and Intelligence Summaries are contained in F. S. Regs., Part II. and the Staff Manual respectively. Title pages will be prepared in manuscript.

Place	Date	Hour	Summary of Events and Information	Remarks and references to Appendices
LEMPIRE SECTOR	OCT 17		VENDHUILE Tr. Mr. were firing at GOULECOURT Tr. Situation quiet. 4500 rds fired harassing fire on tracks and A&C.	Appx 2nd
	18		On footbridge across ST QUENTIN CANAL at S.26.a.3.1 harassing fire during night standed at RONSOY at hour.	Appx 27th
	19th		7500 rds fired at Tracks & rail junctions 1-8	Appx 1st
	20th		Situation normal. 2nd Lt [?] now in charge. Coys during day new gun posts BREAD LANE	Appx 2nd
		3.0L	Concentrated shoot at Cable Tr. M.G. & 10 mounted. TMs & MGs from guns at WT MG by horseshoe Lake P.C. S.34. Gun at Wt MG by horseshoe Lake fired 10,000 rds fairly heavy shell but no casualties. 1500 rds fired harassing fire at S.26.a.3	Appx 2nd
	21st		Situation normal. 500 shells went in S.25.a + 1500 rds harassing Lt Stewart + 2 Lt Kelly	Appx 2nd
			HQ. to BONY. Left Lempire arrived in Bony 4pm	Appx 2nd
	22nd		Situation normal. 870 rds on Ridge S.21 + 1570 rds on QUENNEMONT FARM. 2 heavy machine guns posted at A.20.c SO.9.5. It Stewart relieved It Stewart	Appx 1st

WAR DIARY or INTELLIGENCE SUMMARY

Army Form C. 2118.

Place: LEMPIRE SECTOR

Date	Hour	Summary of Events and Information	Remarks
Oct 23rd		Situation normal. 500 whizz bangs on VENDHUILE that [illegible]	
		on LONE TREE TR. 10 R [illegible] SW but station [illegible] [illegible]	
		[illegible] hrs later.	
24th		[illegible] normal. 500 [illegible] on [illegible] 250 on VENDHUILE	
		750 whizz on trench [illegible] T14 [illegible]	
25th		[illegible] normal. 500 whizz [illegible] with [illegible] on VENDHUILE [illegible]	
26th		[illegible] 1500 whizz on LIMONE TR [illegible] on VENDHUILE	
		[illegible] 3 min [illegible] [illegible] [illegible] on LITTLE PRIEL [illegible]	
		[illegible] with [illegible] [illegible] [illegible] [illegible] known to attach to [illegible]	
		[illegible] 5th [illegible] [illegible]	
27th		Situation normal. [illegible] shelling of [illegible] T13 + T14 on BEEK KNOLL	
		TR from 5 pm to 5.10 pm. 40,000 on [illegible] [illegible] attack of [illegible] by [illegible] guns	
28th		Activity [illegible] McGr [illegible] 500-5 pm [illegible] enemy attacked [illegible] boundary [illegible] and	
		[illegible] [illegible] [illegible] [illegible] 25 each on CLAYMORE TR, 300 [illegible] [illegible] [illegible]	
		[illegible] BONY with [illegible] [illegible] [illegible]	
29th		Situation [illegible] [illegible] [illegible] [illegible] CLAYMORE TR 250 on [illegible] F.A	

164 M.G. Coy

WAR DIARY
or
INTELLIGENCE SUMMARY.
(Erase heading not required.)

Army Form C. 2118.

Place	Date	Hour	Summary of Events and Information	Remarks and references to Appendices
LEMPIRE SECTOR	Oct 28th		No 3 Sect relieved No 4 Section in former battery positions & have given harassing fire. 96 M.G.'s per sec out Bosh Salient. In winner from 166 Bde	None
	30th		Relief carried out by 301st Div 24/10/17. Check kept and 2700 S.A.A. being fired at 500 rounds per hour	None
	31st		Moved to BONY	None
	Nov 1st		Situation normal. 2500 Rounds of Russian Trench 500 rds on BONY - Rt. HT normal Relief of Indirect 6th & 115 M.G. Coy Relief completed by 6.15 M.G. Coy moved to billets at TINCOURT by 2.55 hrs. Coy moved to billets	None

W. Wright
2nd Lieut
p/c O.C.
Every 164th M.G. Coy

164/55

Confidential

War Diary
for
November 1917

164, M. Gun. Coy.

Vol 22

164 M.G. Coy

Army Form C. 2118.

WAR DIARY
INTELLIGENCE SUMMARY

Place	Date	Hour	Summary of Events and Information	Remarks and references to Appendices
LEMPIRE Sub sector	1917 Nov. 1		Situation normal. Company relieved by 165th Machine Gun Coy	
		7.35 p.m.	Relief complete. Company marched by sections to billets at	
			TINCOURT.	
TINCOURT	2		Company training	
	3		Company training	
	4		Company training. Major Crawford proceeded on leave. Lieut. Clark assumed command of the Company	
	5		Company training	
	6		Company training	
	7		Company training	
	8		Company training	
	9		Company training	
	10		Company training	
	11		Church Parade	
	12		Company training	
	13		Company training. Route March. 2/Lt D.F. HARVEY (M.C.) joined Company.	

Army Form C. 2118.

WAR DIARY
or
INTELLIGENCE SUMMARY.

(Erase heading not required.)

2

Place	Date	Hour	Summary of Events and Information	Remarks and references to Appendices
TINCOURT	1917 Nov. 14		Company training. No.2 Section at practice attack firing at LONGAVESNES.	Aff.
	15		Company training. 2/Lt P.J.BENNETT joined Company	Aff.
	16		Recd of 165th Machine Gun Company on the Right Brigade Sector. Disposition of Guns:-	Aff.
			No.1 Section: 2/Lt Nutterton. ISLAND TRAVERSE
			EGG POST.
			FREECHALL POST
			No.2 Section: 2/Lt Harvey. BASSE BOULOGNE
			CAT POST
			BROCK POST
			DUNCAN POST
			No.3 Section: 2/Lt Dixon. GRAFTON POST (2 guns)
			EAGLE QUARRY.
			MALASSISE ROAD
			CRUCIFORM TRENCH

Army Form C. 2118.

WAR DIARY
or
INTELLIGENCE SUMMARY.
(Erase heading not required.)

Instructions regarding War Diaries and Intelligence Summaries are contained in F. S. Regs., Part II. and the Staff Manual respectively. Title pages will be prepared in manuscript.

3

Place	Date	Hour	Summary of Events and Information	Remarks and references to Appendices
LEMPIRE Sur-du-doi	1917 Nov 16	9.30 p.m	4 Guns under O.C. 196¼ M.G. Company Relief Complete. Situation quiet.	96.
	17		8500 Rounds fired on gaps in enemy wire near the front edge GILLEMONT FARM.	96.
	18		At 6.25 am a large enemy barrage party attacked GILLEMONT POST after heavy T.M. and Artillery bombardments. But here at once driven back by a counter attack. Casualties 1 O.R. killed and 4 O.R. wounded. Casualties were inflicted on the Garrison at CPT POST and at GILLEMONT POST. Heavy casualties were inflicted on the enemy. 15,500 rounds fired on gaps in enemy wire.	96. ⁊J⁊⁊ 96.⁊⁊⁊J-⁊
	19		Situation rather Quiet. Occasional shelling of TOMBOIS FARM. 8500 rounds fired on gaps in enemy wire. At midnight the Gun teams moved into position in readiness for the operations on the 20th inst. — the method of the distribution of the guns were as follows —	96.
	20			96.

WAR DIARY or INTELLIGENCE SUMMARY

Army Form C. 2118.

Place	Date	Hour	Summary of Events and Information	Remarks and references to Appendices
KEMPIRE Sur actor	1917 Nov 20		BIRD GROUP — 8 guns under 2/Lt. Discombe and Bennett.	
			CAUSEWAY GROUP — 4 guns under 2/Lt. Little.	
			BRITTEN GROUP — 4 guns attached from 106th Machine Gun Company	
			STONE GROUP — 4 guns attached from 106th Machine Gun Company	
			These 20 guns were engaged on barrage tasks	
			A sub section (M.G.C.) under 2/Lt Manning was detailed to go forward with the 11th R. Lancs. R. A team from the 116th Coy. was attached to the 13th Cheshire R. and another to the 12th S. Lan. Rgs. so that for guns being under 2/Lt. Little.	
		At 2 a.m.	The guns were in position for the barrage. It was felt that the 14th R.W. Kent R. would assault and capture the enemy front line from HOOT HILL to CROOS RIDGE, 3 minutes later our line was to push northwards and ease. GUTMONT CRESCENT was to remain held. The 11th Liverpool R. and 2/5th Lancs Fus. assaulted Ciprene and our South-wards to join up with 1/4th Lancs. R.	
		6.20 a.m.	Zero hour was at 6.20 a.m. and at 6.22 a.m. the 1/4th Lancs. R. barrage to go forward.	

Army Form C. 2118.

WAR DIARY
or
INTELLIGENCE SUMMARY.
(Erase heading not required.)

5th

Place	Date	Hour	Summary of Events and Information	Remarks and references to Appendices
LEMPIRE Sub-sector	1917 Nov 20th		to No 2 Section under 2/Lt. Stanley. The enemy was found to be holding his front line in force, and although we got over our objectives he after many attempts was unsuccessful in our original front line. The attack on the KNOLL was unsuccessful. Our casualties were – 2/Lt Harvey, Killed, and 5 O.R's wounded. The Guns in the Barrage kept up their fire in cooperation with the T.M.'s and Artillery. From 4.30 p.m. – 4.50 p.m. the guns at BIRD, STONE and BRYTAN fired on their S.O.S. lines. In all 33,500 rounds were fired by our guns during Barrage work.	H.6
	21		After the heavy fighting in the morning, the situation became very quiet. Situation quiet – 9000 rounds fired in area behind the KNOLL and Factories and roads to FINS a.m. and a. Redistribution of actions	H.6
	22		Situation normal. Shelling of CAT POST – 1 O.R. killed and 1 O.R. wounded. 9500 rounds fired on roads and tracks behind enemy lines and also on area behind KNOLL. Major Crawford relieved from Leave and resumed Command of the Company.	H.6

Army Form C. 2118.

WAR DIARY
or
INTELLIGENCE SUMMARY.
(Erase heading not required.)

Instructions regarding War Diaries and Intelligence Summaries are contained in F. S. Regs., Part II. and the Staff Manual respectively. Title pages will be prepared in manuscript.

Place	Date	Hour	Summary of Events and Information	Remarks and references to Appendices
LEMPIRE Schools	Nov 23		Church Parade. Company formed.	
			Received [illegible] orders to take over Trenches.	
TINCOURT	24		Company Training	
	25		Drill & Rifle [illegible]	
		afternoon	[illegible]	
			A/Lieut W. FERGUSSON joined from 2nd Bn	
	26		Company Training. Posted to Coy in 8th [illegible]	
	27		Company Training	
	28		Lieut B. SYNGE on "Kemp 2nd Lieut" [illegible]	
			Services [illegible] held	
		11.50 p.m.	Company ordered to be ready to move	
	29		[illegible] attack [illegible]	
	30	10 a.m.	Company [illegible] to entrain	
		2.25 p.m.	[illegible]	
		11.15 a.m.	[illegible]	

Army Form C. 2118.

WAR DIARY
or
INTELLIGENCE SUMMARY.
(Erase heading not required.)

Place	Date	Hour	Summary of Events and Information	Remarks and references to Appendices
LEMPIRE Sub sector	1917 Nov 30		Ref. in Rains later by No. 3 N.H Stations. The actions reports to 16st Infantry Brigade and now changed as follows: 4 Guns under 2/Lt Dixon: X. 26. C. 58. 75 X. 26. C. 7. 7 F. 2. a. 2. 8 F. 2. a. 3. 9. 2 Guns under 2/Lt Bennett: F. 1. d. 6. 4 2 Guns under 2/Lt Aitken: X. 13. d. 0.4 X. 19. E. 2. 1 6 Guns under 2/Lt Orme: X. 25. B. 75. 20 X. 25. d. 3. 7 X. 26. c. 1. 9. X. 26. c. 3. 4 X. 19. c. 5. 4. 1 Gun in reserve at Batt. H.Q. at X.26.c.3.6 Advanced Company Headquarters not established in E. 12. central. S Crawford Major O.C. 164th M.G.C.	A.

SECRET.

BATTLE ORDER NO. BY 7TH BATTALION C.E.F.

In connection with forthcoming operations the following
arrangements have been made:-

1. SECRECY.
All precautions must be taken to ensure that a strict secrecy
will be strictly observed.

2. MACHINE GUN BARRAGE FIRING.
[illegible] are being placed in position at the disposal
of 1/4th S. [illegible]. At ZERO hour information [illegible] be forwarded in
to rear in CIPHER. These guns will move forward under orders of
Officer Commanding 1/4th S. [illegible].

16th Machine Gun Company [illegible] attack gun positions are also here to
[illegible] of 1/4th [illegible] R, and 7/4th [illegible]. These guns
will move forward under orders of O.C. Battalions respectively.
1/4th S. [illegible] R will at ZERO as arranged it on conditions to each
on other forward.

Machine gun teams with assaulting parties will act as the Officers
Commanding the Battalions to which they are attached, inform, at night
it may arise, at these the places to be noted is arranged between Officers
Commanding 16th Machine Gun Company and Officers Commanding Battalions
concerned.

A further section of machine guns may be ordered forward on the
SOUTH front. This section will come from 21st Group. No interruption
or modification of barrage and by this section will take place until the
order to move is required.

3. MACHINE GUNS must not however be involved in hand to hand fighting at the
outset. They will only move forward with the rear of assaulting waves.

4. BARRAGE GUN BARRAGE
The advance of the infantry will be covered by indirect machine gun
barrage of 40 guns.

Details of the fire of the different groups from ZERO onwards and of
their normal S.O.S. lines will be communicated later.

5. SMOKE AND THERMIT.
With the object of preventing enemy observation whilst our infantry
are advancing on THE KNOLL, a detachment of No. 1 Special Co, R.E. will,
from positions in TARA TRENCH, fire smoke and Thermit shells on the area
KNOLL - TRENCH LANE - N. of TRENCH SYSTEM from ZERO plus 19 min. to ZERO plus
34 min. If the wind is unfavourable, only Thermit will be fired.

6. CO-OPERATION WITH AIRCRAFT (CONTACT and ANTI-COUNTER-ATTACK AEROPLANES).

(a) MARKING.
Planes will be marked with a black band under right lower wing, continued into a streamer.

View from)
ground)

(b) CONTACT M/C.
To show most advanced line, Infantry will lit WHITE FLARES, to be lit in the bottom of a trench or behind a parapet.

The signal for lighting flares will be a white Very Light fired from the aeroplane. The Klaxon Horn will also be used by the aeroplane sounding a series of "K's" in Morse. The Klaxon, however, may not always be audible. As this is the only occasion on which White Very Lights will be fired from the air, flares must be lit immediately by the most advanced infantry on seeing this signal.

For the HILL FRONT PARK attack, contact aeroplane will be up from ZERO plus 30 minutes to ZERO plus 6 minutes.

For the KNOLL attack contact aeroplane will be up from ZERO plus 60 minutes to ZERO plus 80 minutes.

(c) ANTI-COUNTER-ATTACK M/C.
From ZERO plus 30 minutes an anti-counter attack aeroplane will be over the line, to watch for enemy troops massing for counter-attack. This machine will remain up until ZERO plus 3 hours. Other anti-counter attack patrols will keep on this duty continually throughout the day, flying at about 1,500 feet.

The signal from anti-counter attack aeroplane will be a smoke bomb dropped vertically over the target. The smoke bomb will burst about 100 feet below the machine into a White Parachute Flare, which descends slowly leaving a trail of brown smoke about 1 foot broad behind it.

On seeing the above signal, Artillery and Machine Gun barrages will be opened immediately without further orders on all hostile assemblies in that vicinity.

7.
(a) WIRE COMMUNICATIONS.
Wires laid from Brigade to Battalion Battle Headquarters.

Prior to ZERO. Messages will be sent by runner.
Only in case of emergency may the wires be used, and then only FULL STRENGTH.

AFTER ZERO. Communications will be by Fullerphones.
Telephone will only be used in case of emergency necessity, and then only by Officers.
Battalions will run out lines to companies themselves as soon as possible after ZERO. Brigade signals will issue necessary cable for this purpose.

(b) RUNNERS.

(b) [illegible]
[illegible] 'Z' day [illegible] Brigade [illegible] will be established at

Post No. 1 ... T.17.[illegible] ([illegible]).

Post No. 2 ... T.17.[illegible] ([illegible]).

(c) [illegible]

[illegible] will be as follows:-

[illegible] .... [illegible]

P.O.W. [illegible] .... [illegible]
[illegible]

7. [illegible]

(a) Location of [illegible]:

Main Brigade [illegible] at [illegible], T.[illegible] [illegible]
Water [illegible]

Advanced Brigade [illegible] at
[illegible] Road, T.[illegible] [illegible]
Water [illegible]
[illegible] ROAD, T.11.b.[illegible] [illegible]
Water [illegible]

[illegible] Dump, [illegible] ROAD ([illegible]) [illegible]
[illegible]
[illegible]

Units may draw on the Brigade [illegible] without reference to the Brigade.

(b) RATIONS.
Two day's rations, including Rum and [illegible], will be issued to all Units at Refilling Point on 'Y' day.

On 'Z' day every man will go forward with a full 24 hours rations.

(c) WATER.
Sufficient water in petrol tins will be held in [illegible] for filling water bottles for all men going over.

8. MEDICAL ARRANGEMENTS.

REGIMENTAL AID POSTS.

[illegible] (T.17.[illegible]) for Battalion [illegible] FARM.
[illegible] FARM (T.11.b.[illegible]) for 2 Battalions assaulting the [illegible].
The above R.A.Ps. are also available for the 4th Battalion [illegible] Inf. Bde., and the Battalion of [illegible] Inf. Bde. in Brigade Reserve to [illegible] Inf. Bde.

[illegible] ROAD (T.[illegible]) for Battalion in [illegible] Sub-sector.

4.

OBSERVATION POSTS:

No. 17 Copse (R. & a. L.G.)
SWAIN TRENCH ROAD (T. M., L. & G.)

ADVANCED DRESSING STATION

LESBŒUFS (G, 15 c. 8.)

MARCHING WOUNDED.

WALKING WOUNDED WILL BE CLEARED TO DIVISION AID POSTS OF TO
THE ADVANCED DRESSING STATION.

[signature]

O.C. 169th Machine Gun Company.

W. L. W.

Issued to:-

Copy No. 1 - C.O.
2 - Bn. In Support.
3 - 169th Inf. Bde.
4 - Maj Mary.
5 - 2/Lt. Brown.
6 - 2/Lt. Wilberton.
7 - 2/Lt. Harvey.
8 - 2/Lt. Hewitt.

S E C R E T.   Copy No. [illegible]

[illegible] MACHINE GUN COMPANY ORDER No. [illegible]

Ref. Maps 57c. N.E. 1/20,000.   [illegible] November, 19[illegible].
[illegible], 1/20,000.

---

1. The [illegible] Infantry Brigade will carry out the following operation.

2. At ZERO plus [illegible] minutes the 1/4th [illegible] Lancs. R. will assault and capture the enemy front and support lines from [illegible] LANE to [illegible] LANE (inclusive). [illegible] TRENCH - [illegible] TRENCH will be consolidated as the main line of resistance, and [illegible] LONE [illegible] will be occupied as a forward line of observation, with strong points of resistance to break up hostile counter attacks.

At ZERO plus 15 minutes 1/4th [illegible] Lancs. R. will push northwards and clear [illegible] as far north as [illegible] LANE where temporary block will be established.

At ZERO plus [illegible] minutes 1/5th L'pool R. and [illegible] Lancs. Fus. will assault and capture the [illegible] area.

1/5th L'pool R. will push southwards along LONE [illegible] and [illegible] TRENCH until touch is gained with 1/4th [illegible] Lancs. R. They will consolidate [illegible] TRENCH - [illegible] TRENCH as a main line of resistance. LONE [illegible] TRENCH - [illegible] TRENCH to [illegible] TRENCH - [illegible] will be held as a forward line of observation, with strong points to break up hostile counter attacks.

[illegible] Lancs. Fus. will consolidate [illegible] TRENCH - [illegible] TRENCH as a main line of defence, with forward posts in [illegible] and, if possible, in the area between [illegible] TRENCH and [illegible].

As soon as the situation permits 1/4th [illegible] Lancs. R. will connect up [illegible] TRENCH with [illegible] - [illegible], and make good [illegible] TRENCH and [illegible] AVENUE.

3. The assaulting Infantry will be supported by Artillery, Trench Mortars and a Machine Gun barrage of [illegible] guns, of which [illegible] are under the control of [illegible] Machine Gun Company. They are disposed as follows:-

[illegible] GROUP. 8 guns, Nos. 3 and 4 Sections, under 2/Lt. [illegible] and 2/Lt. [illegible].

[illegible] GROUP. 4 Guns No. 1 Section under 2/Lt. [illegible].

[illegible] GROUP. 4 guns attached from [illegible] Machine Gun Company.

Guns will take up their barrage positions on "Y" day. All must be in position, with guns laid on barrage lines, by [illegible] a.m. on "Z" day.

These guns will open fire on Barrage and S.O.S. lines as per programme already issued. They will be in telephone communication with Advanced Company Headquarters.

2.

All guns must fire with TNT glycerine in the barrel casing. Coolant must be always kept on the gun.

4. When the captured positions have been consolidated, No. 2 Section will go forward and take up positions in the main defensive line.

The Section will be disposed as follows:-

Dug-out in CITY ROAD:-
    2 guns attached to 1/6th R. Lancs. R. under 2/Lt. Harvey.

Dug-out in DUMOIS PARK:-
    1 gun attached to 1/6th L'pool R. under 2/Lt. Scotch.
    1 gun attached to 1/5th Lancs. Reg. under 2/Lt. Scotch.

The Section will be disposed as above before 3 a.m. on "Y" day. The Officers concerned will then report to Advanced Battalion Headquarters.

These guns will only move forward when ordered to do so by the respective Battalion Commanders.

5. When guns are in position their location will be reported to Advanced Company Headquarters at R. & central (1 BRIGADE M.G. Section Headquarters).

6. Some of the guns of No. 2? GROUP may also be ordered to go forward to the MAIN line. These will be under the command of 2/Lt. Bennett.

7. 10 attached men from 1/6th R. Lancs. R. will report to 2/Lt. Harvey before 3 p.m. on "Y" day. Guides will be provided for these to join their teams. At dusk the teams will proceed to their respective dug-outs in CITY ROAD and DUMOIS PARK.

8. All guns, both barrage and those going forward, will come into action with 14 full belt boxes.

9. DRESS. Fighting order. Equipment with valise on back. No haversack. Greatcoats left behind. Two bombs will be carried by each man.

    24 hours' rations will be carried by all ranks.
    Water bottles will be filled.

10. Watches will be synchronised twice at Brigade Battle Headquarters - once at ZERO minus 5 hours and once at ZERO minus 1 hours. An Officer from the M.G. GROUP will report at Brigade Battle Headquarters with 2 watches at the times stated above. A similar will report to 2/Lt. Atherton with signal time at ZERO minus 1 hours.

11. All our bombs will then be used to kill the Infantry at zero and to fire on all other occasions when the situation demands it or when ordered to do so.

12. "X" hr and ZERO hour will be notified later.

13. ACKNOWLEDGE.

Lieut.
Brig. Maj. Perkins 6th Brigade.

Issued at 11.30 a.m.

Copy No. 1 = HQ.
2 = 5th Aus Division.
3 = 6th Inf. Bde.
4 = O.C. 21st COMP.
5 = O.C. 22nd COMP.
6 = O.C. 24th COMP.
7 = Lt. Harvey.
8 = HQs.
9 = War Diary.

CONFIDENTIAL

164/55

War Diary
for
December 1917

164th M. Gun Coy.

Vol 23

104 Machine Gun Company WAR DIARY or INTELLIGENCE SUMMARY. Army Form C. 2118.

December 1917

Place	Date	Hour	Summary of Events and Information	Remarks and references to Appendices
Epehy Sector	1917. Dec 1st	2 a.m.	Advanced Company Headquarters established at RAILWAY CAMP at W.23.c.5.1 The guns at YAUCELETTE FARM (X.13.a.O.4.) reported to Company H.Q. on relief at 12 noon by Canadian M.G. Cavalry. Two guns with A/4 Coy. Also reported and were held in reserve. The guns in the line fired bursts on the enemy during the day. Casualties – 3 other ranks wounded.	
	2nd	6 p.m.	Company relieved by 110th and 64th Machine Gun Companies. Proceeded by route march to KNEELS at HAMEL arriving at 11 p.m.	
HAMEL	3rd		Company training. Cleaning guns.	
do	4th		Company training.	
EPEHY Sector		2:15 p.m.	8 guns under O.C. Coy proceeded to report to H.Q. 196th Machine Gun Company at VILLERS FAUCON. Four guns on each of roads for positions along LEMPIRE – EPEHY Road under OC Coy – OC MALASSISE FARM positions of guns:– F.8.c.40.65, F.8.c.55.00, F.9.c.28.15, F.9.c.28.15, F.15.a.70.75.	

Army Form C. 2118.

WAR DIARY
or
INTELLIGENCE SUMMARY.

(Erase heading not required.)

Instructions regarding War Diaries and Intelligence Summaries are contained in F. S. Regs., Part II, and the Staff Manual respectively. Title pages will be prepared in manuscript.

Place	Date	Hour	Summary of Events and Information	Remarks and references to Appendices
VILLERS FAUCON	1917 Dec 5th	11.30 a.m	Four guns under 2/Lt Addison reported at 55th Division H.Q at VILLERS FAUCON and remained here	
EPEHY Sector	6th	6 a.m	Four guns under 2/Lt Bennett occupied positions in LEMPIRE - RONSSOY area in defences under command of G.O.C in Command, 2nd Dublin Fusiliers	
HAMEL		9.30 a.m	Headquarters and one section C/O HAMEL on and proceeded by route march to FLAMICOURT (near PÉRONNE) arriving there at 12 noon	
FLAMICOURT	7th		10 other ranks reinforcements joined Company, also 2/Lt J.L. JACK, reinforcement.	
	8th	11 a.m.	Three sections and transport joined Company at FLAMICOURT	
			Company entrained at FLAMICOURT - PÉRONNE and detrained at BEAUMETZ - LES - LOGES at 9 p.m.	
			Proceeded by route march to billets at HABARCQ	
HABARCQ	9th	12.30 a.m	The transport proceeded from FLAMICOURT to HABARCQ by road	
	10th		Company proceeded by route march to BETHENCOURT occupying billets here	
	11th		Company marched via TINQUES - CHELERS - VALHUON to CONTEVILLE. Inspected en route by Brig. General C. I. STOCKWELL	
			Company billeted at CONTEVILLE overnight. 11 other ranks reinforcements joined	

Army Form C. 2118.

WAR DIARY
or
INTELLIGENCE SUMMARY.
(Erase heading not required.)

Instructions regarding War Diaries and Intelligence Summaries are contained in F. S. Regs., Part II. and the Staff Manual respectively. Title pages will be prepared in manuscript.

3

Place	Date	Hour	Summary of Events and Information	Remarks and references to Appendices
	1917 Sep 12th		Company marched via HESTRUS - EPS - PETIT ANVIN - FERGUENEUSE to EQUIRRE. Billets fine overnight	
	13th		Company marched via FRUGES to CAPELLE Sur la LYS taking up billets here	
CAPELLE sur la LYS	14th		Inspection by Brig Gen C.I. Stockwell of Company on march through FRUGES. Company training	
			Revt W T HEWINS, Officer reinforcement, reported for duty	
	15th		2/Lt Litherton reported. Company from leave	
	16th		2/Lt Snedding reported. Company from hospital	
	15th		Company training	
	16th		Church Parade - Inspection by CO	
	17th		Company training	
	18th		Company training - Lieut Clarke proceeded on leave to U.K.	
	19th		Company training	
	20th		Company training	
	21st		Company training	
	22nd		Company training	

Army Form C. 2118.

WAR DIARY
or
INTELLIGENCE SUMMARY.
(Erase heading not required.)

Place	Date	Hour	Summary of Events and Information	Remarks and references to Appendices
CAPELLE Sec Le A/S	1917 Dec 23rd		Church Parades. Inspection by C.O.	
	24th		Company training	
	25th		Church Parade - Company proceeded to dinner by 12th Co and Officers of the Company. No training.	
	26th		Company training	
	27th		Company training	
	28th		Company training	
	29th		Company training	
	30th		Company training	
	31st		Company training. Lt. Scaading to 1st Corps Infantry School	

Wm Addison 2/Lt
for Major
Comdg 164th Machine Gun Coy

16th Machine Gun Company

WAR DIARY
or
INTELLIGENCE SUMMARY.
(Erase heading not required.)

Army Form C. 2118.

Instructions regarding War Diaries and Intelligence Summaries are contained in F. S. Regs., Part II. and the Staff Manual respectively. Title pages will be prepared in manuscript.

Place	Date 1918	Hour	Summary of Events and Information	Remarks and references to Appendices
CAPELLE - aux - B - LYS.	Jan. 1		Company received training by Brigadier General Shot, inspection by Section Officers.	
	2		Company Training	
	3		do	
	4		do 2/Lt Clark from leave 2/Lt Pitts from VII Corps School. 1 other rank from leave	
	5		Company Training	
	6		Church Parade. 2/Lt Bennett and 2 N.C.Os. for attachment to 1/4th N. Fus. R. for a month.	
	7		2/Lt PAYMENT (1/4th K.Lpool R.) and 2 N.C.Os (2/5th Lanc Fus) for one months attachment to this Company. Company Training - Tactical exercise - G.O.C. Division wrote Training area whilst exercise was being carried out.	
	8		Company Training - Sectional Tactical Exercises - Baths at COYECQUE. 1 other rank reinforcement.	
	9		Company Training - Route March and reconnaissance of 2/Lt Clark's line.	

Army Form C. 2118.

WAR DIARY
or
INTELLIGENCE SUMMARY.
(Erase heading not required.)

January 1918.

Place	Date 1918	Hour	Summary of Events and Information	Remarks and references to Appendices
	Jan. 10.		Company Training - Firing on Range.	
	11.		Company Training - Company Tactical Scheme.	
	12.		Company Training - Firing on Range continued with one tactical exercise.	
	13.		Church Parade - Inspection by Co. and Section Officers.	
	14.		D.A.G.O. visited Company for training three days for reconnaissance in training and tactical exercises.	
			Company Training - Tactical exercises - 1 anti-section attached to 1/1st N.Lancs.R. for tactical exercises which were cancelled owing to weather conditions.	
	15.		Company training - Tactical exercises. 1 subs. section (No.14) attached to 2/5th Lancs Fus for tactical exercise. 1 subs. section (No.1) attached to 1/1st Black R. to scheme, but cancelled owing to weather.	
	16.		Company training - Tactical exercises abandoned on account of weather. 2/Lt. Rayment (1/1st K.L.Fus.R.) and 2 other ranks (2/5th Lancs. Fus.) returned to their units, whilst Off. Bennett and John James returned to duty with this company after attachment to 1/1st N.Lancs.R.	
CAPELLE - sur - LYS				

WAR DIARY
or
INTELLIGENCE SUMMARY.
(Erase heading not required.)

Army Form C. 2118.

January 1918

Place	Date	Hour	Summary of Events and Information	Remarks and references to Appendices
CAPELLE-OUEST R-L/S	1918 Jan 17.		Firing on Range. Aiming Anti-Aircraft Sights. Revolver Practice.	
	18		- do -	
	19.		Inspection of Brigade by 1st Army Commander near CAYEUX at 11 a.m. Presentation of medal ribbons to winners of awards. Sgt Burns & No.	
			Company presented with Military Medal Ribbon. Church Parades. Inspection of billets by Co.	
	20.			
	21.		Company Training - Revolver practice. Paths for Company at CAYEUX. Lecture by the Brigadier General Commanding on Principles of Fire Action.	
	22		Company Training - Route March continued with Reconnaissance by Officers and Sergeants.	
	23.		Company Training - Firing on Range with guns and Revolvers. No. 2 Section attached to 1st/4th Hoss R. for schemes.	
	24		Section Tactical Exercises continued with Range firing. Rifle & Revolver. Inspection by M.O. Lt. Knox R.	
	25		Company Training - Passing of Pigeons. No. 1 Section attached to 1st/8 R of R trench to trench attack scheme. No. 2 Section	

Army Form C. 2118.

WAR DIARY
or
INTELLIGENCE SUMMARY.
(Erase heading not required.)

of January 1918

Place	Date 1918	Hour	Summary of Events and Information	Remarks and references to Appendices
CAPELLE - 5/5 - 6 - 5/5	Jan 25 (cont.)		attached to 1/8 Bn. R.R. for tactical scheme.	
			2/Lt. T.T. Orme returned from leave	
	26		Company Training - Section tactical scheme. 5 other ranks reinforcements	
	27		Church Parade. Inspection of billets by O.C.	
	28		Company Training - Drill with face animals on Range.	
			2/Lt. Hayden proceeded on leave	
	29		Company Training - Baths and disinfector of clothing and blankets at Bomy.	
	30		Company Training - Drill with face animals and practicing "coming into Action" and "Firing". Lecture by Brigade Major on "Work".	
	31		Company Training - Route March. CAPELLE - COYECQUE - DOHEM - DELETTE - CAPELLE.	

31. Janu. 1918.

J. Crawford
Major
Cmdg. 154th M.G. Coy

Confidential

War Diary

for

February 1918

164th M.G. Gun Coy.

www.ingramcontent.com/pod-product-compliance
Lightning Source LLC
Chambersburg PA
CBHW081411160426
43193CB00013B/2157